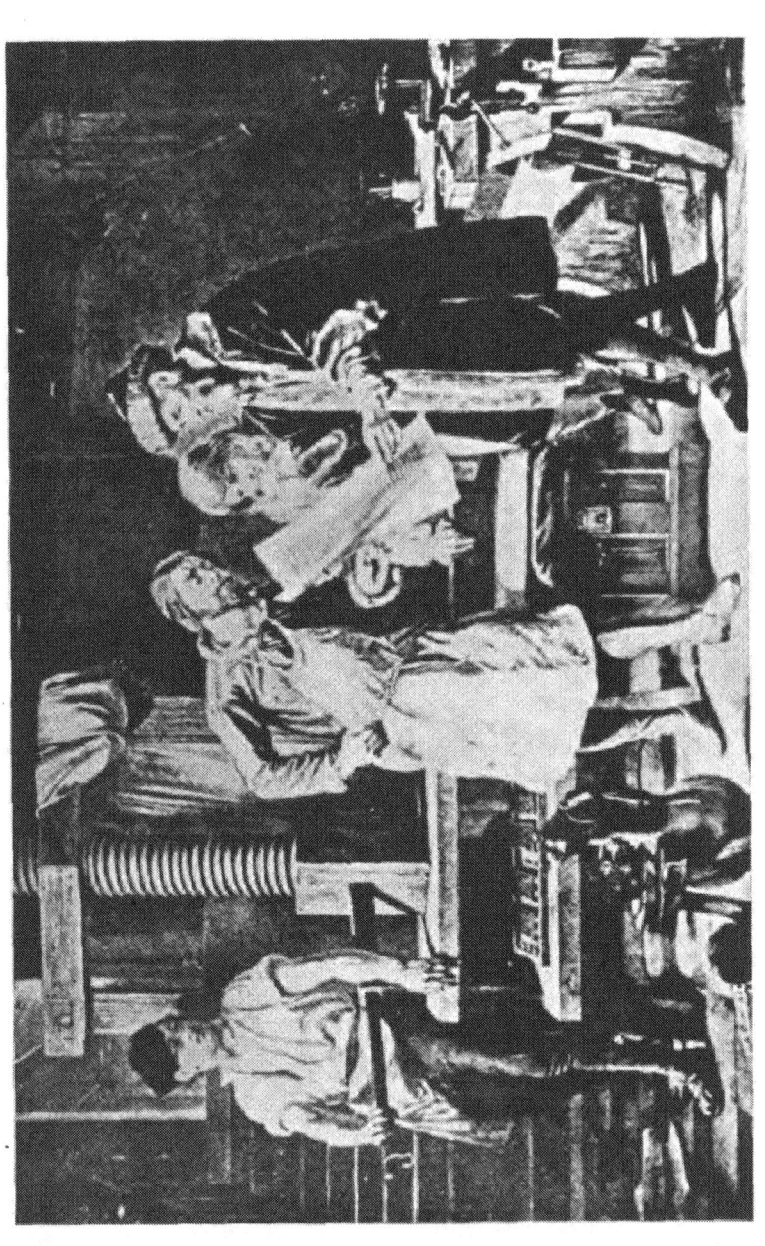

PROOFREADING *and* PUNCTUATION : : : : : :

By ADÈLE MILLICENT SMITH

FORMERLY SECRETARY TO THE PRESIDENT AND INSTRUCTOR IN PROOFREADING, DREXEL INSTITUTE, AND AUTHOR OF "PRINTING AND WRITING MATERIALS," "EXERCISES IN PROOFREADING," AND "EXERCISES IN PUNCTUATION."

SEVENTH EDITION

PHILADELPHIA
PUBLISHED BY THE AUTHOR
1920

PREFACE

THE need of a manual of ready reference, embodying the information necessary in ordinary proof-reading, has led to the preparation of the present volume. The book is designed for use in schools in which proof-reading and a general knowledge of the processes involved in the preparations for printing are made a part of the curriculum, and as an aid to the non-professional proof-reader.

To facilitate reference, the proof-marks have been classified.

In the chapters on Type-founding and Sizes and Styles of Type, accuracy has been secured through the kind assistance of Mr. W. Ross Wilson, Manager American Type-Founders Company. Valuable information in regard to the history and processes of Typesetting has been furnished by Mr. Philip T. Dodge, President of the Mergenthaler Linotype Company, New York, and Mr. Talbert Lanston, of the Lanston Monotype Machine Company, Washington, D. C.

For the descriptions of the processes of paper-making and the folding of the sheets for binding, acknowledgments are due to Mr. A. B. Daniels, of the L. L. Brown Paper Company, Adams, Massachusetts; Mr. H. A. Moses, of the Mittineague Paper Company, Mittineague, Massachusetts; Mr. A. E. Whiting, of the Whiting Paper Company; Mr. J. Shoemaker, of the J. B. Lippincott Company; Mr. Charles R. Graham, of the Historical Publishing Company; Messrs. Irwin N. Megargee & Company; and the Moore & White Company, of Philadelphia.

The information given under Reproductive Processes has been obtained through the kindness of the Avil Printing Company, the Phototype Engraving Company, the editors of the New York World and the New York Journal, and the edit rs of the Evening Bulletin and the Sunday Press of Philadelphia, who kindly afforded the author the opportunity for a complete inspection of the work of their respective mechanical departments.

In the preparation of the Section on Punctuation, much help has been derived from Mr. Theodore L. De Vinne's recent book on Correct Composition, and the well-known works on the subject by Marshall T. Bigelow and John Wilson.

To Frau Hedwig Neuhaus of the Bourse Translation Bureau, Mademoiselle Clara Parigot, Professor Calixto Guitéras, Professor T. E. Comba, and Miss Helen G. Harjes, the author desires to express her high appreciation of the service rendered by the careful reading of the proof of the chapters under foreign languages.

Grateful acknowledgments are made also to President James Mac Alister, Miss May Haggenbotham, Lieut. William L. Bailie, Professor Parke Schoch, Professor H. L. Mason, Miss Alice B. Kroeger, and Miss Alice M. Brennan, of the Drexel Institute, who have so kindly aided in the preparation of the work by their suggestions and encouragement.

A. M. S.

CONTENTS

PROOF-READING AND TYPE-WORK

Chapter		Page
I.	Proof-Marks	1
	List of Proof-Marks	1
	Corrected Proof-Sheets	6
II.	Preparing Copy	10
III.	Reading Proof	13
IV.	Type-Founding	20
V.	Sizes and Styles of Types	26
	The Point System	26
	Types Used in Text Matter	28
	Gradation of Types—Specimens of Regular Sizes of Text-Types	29
	Styles of Types	33
VI.	Typesetting	34
	By Hand	34
	By Machine	35
	Measurement of Type Matter	39
	Leading	40
VII.	Job-Work	42
VIII.	Paper	46
	Paper-making by Machinery	48

CONTENTS

CHAPTER		PAGE
	Paper-making by Hand	53
	Classes of Paper	56
	Sizes of Paper	59
	Folding the Sheets for Binding—Diagrams	60
	Signatures	64
	Make-up of a Book	65
IX.	TECHNICAL TERMS	66

REPRODUCTIVE PROCESSES

I.	STEREOTYPING AND ELECTROTYPING	81
II.	HALF-TONE AND LINE ENGRAVING	86

PUNCTUATION

I.	PUNCTUATION MARKS	93
	The Period	94
II.	THE COLON	97
III.	THE SEMICOLON	100
IV.	THE COMMA	103
V.	THE INTERROGATION POINT	114
	The Exclamation Point	116
VI.	THE DASH	119
VII.	MARKS OF PARENTHESIS	124
	Brackets	126
VIII.	QUOTATION MARKS	129
	The Apostrophe	134

CONTENTS

CHAPTER	PAGE
IX. THE HYPHEN	136
Compound Words	136
Syllabication	140
X. REFERENCE MARKS—MISCELLANEOUS MARKS	144
XI. CAPITAL LETTERS	147
XII. THE ITALIC LETTER	156

ALPHABETS, ACCENTS, DIACRITICAL MARKS, AND DIVISIONS IN THE PRINCIPAL MODERN LANGUAGES

I. DIACRITICAL MARKS—ENGLISH	159
II. FRENCH	161
III. GERMAN	165
IV. SPANISH	169
V. ITALIAN	174

LIST OF ILLUSTRATIONS

	Facing page
GUTENBERG TAKING AN IMPRESSION	*Frontispiece*
PUNCH—DRIVE—MATRIX—MOULD—TYPE	20
BRUCE HAND TYPE-CASTING MACHINE	22
TYPE-CASTING AS PRACTISED BY HAND	24
COMPOSING STICK—GALLEY	34
LANSTON TYPESETTING MACHINE	36
MERGENTHALER TYPESETTING MACHINE (LINOTYPE)	38
STACK OF 52-INCH SUPERCALENDERS—FRONT VIEW	52
HALF-TONE REPRODUCTION—STATUE OF GUTENBERG AT STRASBURG	86
REPRODUCTION FROM LINE PLATE—OLD WOODEN PRINTING-PRESS OF 1508	88

Proof-Reading and Punctuation

PROOF-READING AND TYPE-WORK

CHAPTER I

PROOF-MARKS

The following is a complete list of the proof-marks in common use. An example of the use of each is given in the two pages of Corrected Proof-Sheets, and directions concerning marks that might be improperly employed will be found under READING PROOF.

1. KINDS OF LETTERS

≡   Three horizontal lines under a word or a letter—print in capitals (*caps*).

=   Two horizontal lines under a word or a letter—print in small capitals (*s. caps, sm. c.*).

—   One horizontal line under a word or a letter—change roman to italic, or italic to roman.

l. c.—*Lower case*—change capitals or small capitals to small letters.

w. f.—*Wrong font*—change letter or letters to proper size or style.

2. CHANGE OF MATTER

Dele—Take out

Stet—Let stand.

Used when matter in the proof has been expunged and the reader afterwards decides to let it remain. A line of dots is placed under the word or words stricken out.

3. CHANGE OR INSERT LETTER OR PUNCTUATION MARK

Ligature—print as a diphthong, ligature, or as a single character; thus, *æ, fl,* means print æ, fl.

Insert superior character, such as the apostrophe, quotation marks, etc

4. POSITION

Lower word, letter, or character.

Elevate word, letter, or character.

The direction of the angles indicates the position in which the word, letter, or character is to be placed.

Bring word or words farther to the right.

Bring word or words farther to the left

Bring word or words to the beginning of the line; also, make a new paragraph.

Indent

Reverse letter.

Straighten lateral margin.

5. Spacing

⌒ Less space between letters.

※ More space between words.

⁄ Less space between words.

lead More space between lines.

ᵭ *lead* Less space between lines.

6. Transposition

$\overset{3}{\text{Words}}$—$\overset{2}{beautiful}$ $\overset{1}{and}$ $bright.$

The words to be transposed may be enclosed and a line drawn from them to the place where they are to be inserted; if the order of the words is to be changed, they may be numbered as above indicated, and *tr.* written in the margin.

Letters—fre̸ind, mov̸e̸!

The transposition of letters may be indicated in either of the two ways given above; *tr.* must be written in the margin.

Lines.

When several lines are to be transferred, they should all be enclosed and a line drawn from them to the point where they are to be inserted *tr.* should be written in the margin

7. Imperfect Type or Crooked Lines

✗ or ✚ Broken type.

⊥ or ⊥ Depress space or lead.

⸗ Straighten type in words.

≡ or /// or \\\   Straighten crooked lines.

8. Paragraphs

[¶ New paragraph. The first mark is placed in the text, the second in the margin.

⌒ *no* ¶ Continue in same paragraph. The line unites the two portions of the text; *no* ¶ is placed in the margin.

9. New Matter.

Out, s. c.—Words are omitted, see copy.

See copy—New matter to be inserted.

10. Qu., Qy., ?—Query

Used in printing-offices to call attention to a supposed error in the statement of a fact, obsolete spelling, etc.

CORRECTED PROOF-SHEET, No. 1

After passing Povelia the boat will feel the tide with her; and ten minutes more brings one to the landingplace of Malamocco. Quiet and sleepy and clean; the people with a type distinctly their own; very gently and freindly to strangers, but at heart, seeming to say, "We are not Venetians, but Malamochini". There is a piazza and two long broad streets. In the piazza a flagstaff, with Saint Marks Lion in gilt on the top, as a weathercock, looking straight now to Venice, with his paw firmly placed on his evangel. At the foot of the flagstaff is a quaint old well, with the Pisane superscription and coat, per fesse, azure and argent, a lion rampant counterchanged, engraved upon it. Almost all house-doors have dolphins for knockers. You can walk down the main street, where the maize is drying a yellow carpet spread on one side; where the women sit spinning and not chattering; where the dogs bask against the wall and snap at the flies; out by the arch over the Ponte del Borgo, past the gardens made of Venetian mud, till you reach the shore, and look down to the long water avenue of the Adriatic.

Brown: Life on the Lagoons.

like the Venetians, but quiet

(6)

AFTER CORRECTION BY COMPOSITOR

After passing Poveglia the boat will feel the tide with her; and ten minutes more brings one to the landing-place of Malamocco. Quiet and sleepy and clean; the people with a type distinctly their own; very gentle and friendly to strangers, but at heart seeming to say, " We are not Venetians, but Malamocchini". There is a piazza and two long broad streets. In the piazza a flagstaff, with Saint Mark's lion in gilt on the top, as a weathercock, looking now straight to Venice, with his paw firmly placed on his evangel. At the foot of the flagstaff is a quaint old well, with the Pisani superscription and coat, *per fesse*, azure and argent, a lion rampant counterchanged, engraved upon it. Almost all the house-doors have dolphins for knockers. You can walk down the main street, where the maize is drying, a yellow carpet spread on one side; where the women sit spinning and not chattering, like the Venetians, but quiet; where the dogs bask against the wall and snap at the flies; out by the arch over the Ponte del Borgo, past the gardens made of Venetian mud, till you reach the shore, and look down the long water-avenue of the Adriatic.

BROWN: *Life on the Lagoons.*

CORRECTED PROOF-SHEET, No. 2

Nothing could be more delightful than the spring days which we passed in Barcelona. We could appreciate the language of Washington Irving written in 1844. All here is picture and romance. Nothing has given me greater delight than occasional evening drives with some of my diplomatic colleges to those countr-seats or *torres*, as they are called, situated on the slopes of the hills, 2 or three miles from the City, surrounded by groves of oranges, citrons, figs, and pomegranates, with gay gardens terraced with flowers and fountains. . . ."

Barcelona become a city of trafic and manufactures since Irvings day and can hardly merit now the description of Cervantes, "flor de las bellas ciudades del mundo, the flower of the beautiful cities of the world, but it is still grand, beautiful and captivating. In Barcelona besides the English Church, who sechaplain attends British ships in the harbour, their are missions of the Swiss church with chapel and schools, a Weslyan mission, and several walls walls in the suburbs of Gracia, where where the Plymouth brethren hold and support meetings.

STODDARD: *Spanish Cities.*

AFTER CORRECTION BY COMPOSITOR

Nothing could be more delightful than the spring days which we passed in Barcelona. We could appreciate the language of Washington Irving written in 1844: "All here is picture and romance. Nothing has given me greater delight than occasional evening drives with some of my diplomatic colleagues to those country-seats or *torres,* as they are called, situated on the slopes of the hills, two or three miles from the city, surrounded by groves of oranges, citrons, figs, and pomegranates, with terraced gardens gay with flowers and fountains. . . ." Barcelona has become a city of traffic and manufacture since Irving's day and can hardly merit now the description of Cervantes, " flor de las bellas ciudades del mundo", the flower of the beautiful cities of the world, but it is still grand, beautiful, and captivating.

In Barcelona besides the English Church, whose chaplain attends British ships in the harbour, there are missions of the Swiss Church with chapel and schools, a Wesleyan mission, and several halls in the suburbs of Gracia, where the Plymouth Brethren hold and support meetings.

STODDARD : *Spanish Cities.*

CHAPTER II

PREPARING COPY

BEFORE either a book or job matter is set in types there should be an understanding between the author or the person ordering and the printer as to the dimensions of the work, the size and style of type to be employed and whether it is to be leaded or solid, as to folios, headlines, initials, side-notes or cut-in notes, the color of the ink, and any other matters pertaining to the special work in hand.

Copy is the first draft of matter sent to the printer. Too much care cannot be given to the preparation of copy. The idea that compositors can decipher any kind of a scrawl given them to set, leads many writers to make the first draft of a work very carelessly; this always causes delay and frequently unsatisfactory results. As the composition progresses, especially if there is much matter to be printed, new ideas naturally suggest themselves to the author, and due allowance should always be made for a few changes; but, as a general rule, before copy is sent to the printer, it should be, as nearly as possible, complete and perfect. The compositor is bound to "follow copy" in word and sentiment, unless there should be instances of punctuation or spelling obviously wrong, which he will, of course, correct.

In the preparation of matter to be printed, careful attention should be given to the following points:

1. *Copy should embody all the ideas* which the writer wishes his work to contain.

2. *The sheets of paper used should be all of one size, and not too large*—either commercial note or letter size is convenient for the compositor to handle. One side of the paper only should be used, and the pages should be carefully numbered, so that, if necessary, they can be separated and given to several workmen. The sheets should contain about the same number of lines; this enables the printer quickly to estimate the amount of matter and the cost of printing.

3. *Copy should be either typewritten or written in a legible hand.* Good typewriting saves both the time and the patience of the compositor. No abbreviations should be employed except for words usually so written, and, so far as possible, interlineations should be avoided. The practice of finishing a word with an illegible scrawl should be shunned; it is expecting too much of a compositor to suppose that he has either the time or the intuition to decipher what an author has not fully expressed.

4. *The spelling of proper names and of technical and scientific terms and the use of capitals and punctuation marks should be in accordance with the best usage of the day.* All references and quotations should be verified by consulting the proper authorities.

5. *The copy should be carefully punctuated.* In manuscript, special care should be taken to indicate

the ends of sentences, as the compositor can thus readily gather the meaning of an author, and the work will, in consequence, be greatly facilitated.

Careful punctuation of the copy is a much more important matter than at first appears. It gives the writer but little trouble to substitute on the proof-sheet one mark for another; but to make the same correction, the workman is obliged to lift out the wrong character and insert the proper mark. In doing this, he may drop out a letter or letters, and there is always danger of his making other errors.

6. *Uniformity should be observed in capitalization, in orthography, and in punctuation.* A word that may or may not be capitalized should not be written sometimes with and sometimes without a capital. Words which have two authorized spellings should appear in only one form in the same work. There is some latitude in punctuation, especially in the use of the comma, but one mode should be adopted and strictly followed throughout the work.

7. *The paragraphing should be indicated in the copy* and not left to the compositor.

8. *Directions written on the copy should be enclosed within circles or curved lines,* in order to separate them from the corrections, and that they may be readily seen. *Page* and *leaf* should not be used synonymously; *leaf* means paper, never printed matter.

CHAPTER III

READING PROOF

THE first proof taken from composed types is "pulled" on a hand-press. This is the "office proof," and is corrected by the proof-reader of the printing-house. Any corrections indicated on this proof must be made by the compositor at his own expense. A clean proof, known as "author's proof," is then drawn and is sent with the manuscript to the author. The first proof received by the author is taken from the types in the galley. Afterwards, if he makes many changes, he usually sees a "revised proof" and a "paged proof." *(Office proof. Author's proof.)*

In book-work, after the author has returned the paged proof and before the type is sent to the foundry to be cast, another proof, called a foundry proof, or "planer," is drawn and carefully read in the printing-office. After the pages are cast, still another proof is taken, known as "plate proof," which the author, if he so desires, may see for final inspection. *(Foundry proof. Plate proof.)*

The reading of proof by a corrector of the press, and especially by an author, implies much more than the mere correction of typographical errors. Careful attention must be given to the spelling, the punctuation, the grammatical construction, the style, and the sentiment; quotations, references, scientific terms, and foreign phrases must be verified.

Apart from the necessary qualifications to do this work well, the chief requisite of a good proof-reader is a keen and quick eye for the detection of errors, without which even extensive knowledge will be of little service.

Author's proof.

First proof, or proof in galley.

1. The copy should be read aloud to the corrector by some person who can pronounce distinctly and with ease every word contained in it. (The corrector holds the proof and the reader the copy.) Considerable practice is necessary to enable even a naturally good reader to follow copy literally. Unless he gives close attention to the wording, he may substitute a similarly sounding word for the one in the copy, as *this* for *these;* articles and conjunctions may be slurred over or omitted altogether; and the plural number of nouns read for the singular, or *vice versâ.*

2. The copyholder should sit at the left of the corrector, so that the latter may easily inspect the copy. All uncommon and difficult proper names should be spelled. At the beginning of each paragraph, after the first, the person who reads should say " Paragraph." If the punctuation has been carefully made in the copy, the marks may be given by the copyholder; otherwise, the corrector will save time by revising the punctuation after the reading.

Corrections.

3. It is best to make corrections in ink. If red ink is used, or any ink which is of a contrasting color with the printed proof, the time of the compositor will be saved, as he can thereby see at a glance the

changes desired. Lead-pencil marks are liable to become blurred and indistinct.

4. Corrections should be made on the blank margin, opposite the lines in which the errors are respectively found, and in exactly the same order in which the latter occur. Corrections are generally separated from each other by oblique lines. Long lines connecting the error with the correction in the margin should be used only when absolutely necessary, for instance, when new matter is to be inserted. The frequent use of such lines tends to confuse the compositor, and necessitates his spending too much time in deciphering the alterations to be made—time which must be paid for by the author.

5. When several errors occur in one line, the changes should be made in the margin nearest the respective errors which they are intended to correct; but these alterations must always be made in exactly the same order in which the mistakes occur.

When there are several errors in one word, it is better to rewrite the whole word correctly than to indicate each change separately.

6. Superior characters, such as the apostrophe, quotation marks, accents, etc., should always be enclosed, as shown in the list of Proof-marks, to prevent their being placed on a range with the letters of the line.

7. If much new matter is to be added, it should be written on another piece of paper and attached to the proof-sheet. If only a few lines are to be inserted, they may be written on the margin of the proof-sheet

Some of the errors which are most likely to escape notice are:

Errors which escape notice.

1. The omission of a letter or syllable, or the substitution of one letter for another, which does not greatly change the outline of the word; as, *constution* for *constitution*, *edifid* for *edified*, *couutry* for *country*.

2. The insertion of a word which is not in the copy and which does not materially alter the sense. This is especially true of articles and conjunctions.

3. The repetition of a syllable or word which ends one line, at the beginning of the next.

4. The substitution of one word for another, which differs from it but slightly in spelling and which sometimes makes sense; as, *wall* for *hall*.

Detecting errors.

After the copy has been read aloud, it is well for the corrector to go through the proof several times, intent each time on finding errors of one particular kind. He should read it through once for the sentiment, then run through it again, noting the spelling and punctuation, and again searching for typographical errors. Inaccuracies are often thus detected which escape attention during the first reading, and with practice this manner of revision becomes easy and takes but little time.

When a query (?, *qu.*, *qy.*) has been made on the proof-sheet by the professional proof-reader (the proof-reader of the printing-house), if the author desires the suggested change, he should make the correction and draw a line through the query. If he wishes the matter to stand as set up, a line through

READING PROOF

the query is sufficient. Queries should never be left standing. Marks should never be rubbed out with an eraser.

The mark meaning "reverse," should be used only when a letter is actually upside down. When one letter is substituted for another, as a *u* for an *n*, or a *p* for a *b*, the correction should be made by placing the proper letter in the margin.

After the corrections indicated in the First or Galley Proof have been made by the compositor, unless the work is short and but few changes have been made, the author should see a Second Proof, or Revise. This not only assures the writer that the desired alterations have all been made, but enables him to prevent others from appearing in the finished work. Unless he has had long experience as a reader of proof, he will always find some mistakes which escaped his notice during the reading of the first proof; experienced readers, however, sometimes fail to detect errors. *Second proof or revised proof.*

When many corrections are made in the Revise, a Second Revise, or a Third Proof, should be asked for before the work goes to press. If the matter in hand is important and difficult, the author should not hesitate to ask for additional proofs until he is satisfied that his work is as nearly as possible perfect.

When matter is to be paged, the author should see a Paged Proof. He should be careful to see that the pages are of equal length; that the register is good, that is, that the pages back against each other *Paged proof.*

properly, the edges exactly coinciding; and he should note any other discrepancies that may occur.

Proof should be corrected as soon as received and returned at once to the printer. When a form is kept standing a long time, the adhesion of the type is weakened, and there is danger of letters falling out. While the proof is in the author's hands, the printer's type is idle, which may prove to him a serious inconvenience. A writer can hardly expect a printer to hurry work, if he keeps the proof-sheets beyond a reasonable time.

<small>Cost of author's corrections.</small> As corrections must be paid for according to the time required to make them, it is the part of wisdom to make as few changes as possible. Authors are frequently surprised at the high charge made for their corrections. This arises partly from the fact that they are ignorant of the amount of time and labor required to make the changes desired. The introduction or elimination of a word or two often necessitates the "overrunning," or readjustment of several lines, and sometimes of all the lines to the end of the paragraph. The author, besides, takes no note of the number of corrections as they are made from time to time; but they are all recorded in the printing-office, and frequently reach in the aggregate an almost incredible amount. The more carefully the manuscript is prepared, the less, of course, will be the charge for corrections.

Expense can be saved by indicating, so far as

possible, all the corrections on one proof, as every additional handling of the type consumes more time, and, consequently increases the cost. In book-work, however, this is not possible, as there are nearly always some details to be changed, up to the final moment when the work is ready to go to press.

The most expensive kind of correction that can be made is to reset matter in type of another size or style. Notes and extracts, which are put in smaller type than the text, should, therefore, always be indicated in the copy.

Corrections should be made in the galley rather than in the paged proof, as in the latter it is often necessary to "overrun," or carry matter from page to page. Changes can be made even after the type is cast, but it is an expensive process. Corrections cost *least* in the galley and *most* in the plate.

CHAPTER IV

TYPE-FOUNDING

FROM the time of the invention of typography until the middle of the sixteenth century, printers made their own type. Many printing-offices had only four or five sizes, and but small quantities of these. After 1550 the casting of types became a distinct business.

Claude Garamond, of Paris, a pupil of Geoffroy Tory, the great French engraver and printer, is known as the "father of letter-founders."

In England, the first founder of note was Joseph Moxon, who began letter-cutting in 1659; but neither Moxon's types nor those of his immediate successors could compare with the type cast in France and Holland. William Caslon, who established a foundry about 1720, had greater success. His work possessed such technical excellence that England soon ceased to purchase type from Holland. This house was controlled by the Caslon family to the fifth generation, and is still successful and flourishing.

In America, type-casting was attempted as early as 1768. The first regular foundry was established by Christopher Sauer, at Germantown, Pennsylvania, about 1772. Several unsuccessful efforts to establish foundries in the United States were made by various

PUNCH.

DRIVE.

MATRIX.

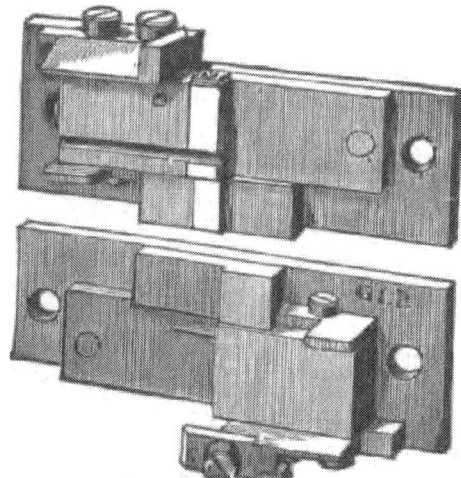

MOULD—SHOWING THE TWO PARTS.

TYPE—SHOWING FACE[1] AND NICK.[2]

persons, among whom was Benjamin Franklin. In 1796 Binney and Ronaldson, of Edinburgh, began the business in Philadelphia. This was the first foundry which lasted for many years. The house was subsequently known as the Johnson Foundry, afterwards as the Mac Kellar, Smiths, and Jordan branch of the American Type-Founders Company. Successful foundries were established, also, in New York, early in the nineteenth century, by Elihu White and D. and G. Bruce.

Until near the middle of the nineteenth century, all type was cast by hand. About 1828 William M. Johnson, of Long Island, made the experiment of casting type by machinery, but his types were too light and porous to be of practical use. In 1838 David Bruce, jr., of New York, took out a patent for a type-casting machine which was more successful. This machine was afterwards improved and was generally adopted by the foundries of the United States; it was gradually introduced, with modifications, into European foundries. *Type-founding by machinery.*

Type-metal is an alloy of melted lead, tin, and antimony, sometimes hardened by an addition of copper or nickel. The large types used for posting-bills are made from close-grained wood, such as box, maple, or pear; for this purpose, types of wood are lighter and cheaper than those made from metal. *Type-metal.*

The tools made before the letter is cast are, first, the Counter-punch and the Punch, or more frequently at the present day, an engraved Master-type; from the punch or the master-type is made the Matrix or *The tools.*

the mould for the letter or face of the type. The *tool* termed the Mould is that which holds the matrix during the process of casting.

The punch-cutter first draws a geometrical framework, on which is determined the position of each line and the height of each character. The beauty of a printed page consists in the apparent precision of the types. The characters must seem uniform in every particular, but some allowance must be made for optical delusions; occasional deviations must also be made, to render each letter pleasing to the eye in any combination with other letters.

The counter-punch. The interior of the letter is not cut out, but the hollow of the letter, or that part of it which does not show black in the printed impression, is formed on steel in high relief. This is the Counter-punch.

The punch. The Punch is made by impressing the counter-punch into the end of a short bar of soft steel. The interior of the letter is thus quickly made at one stroke, and with much neater edges than could be given by cutting. The outer edges are cut away, and the model letter stands in high relief.

The punch is hardened and is forced into a flat, narrow bar of cold-rolled copper. The result is a reverse or sunken imprint of the letter on the punch, which is known as a strike, a drive, or an unjustified matrix. This is carefully finished and becomes the Matrix. The matrix is really the mould for the face

The matrix. of the letter, but it is not the tool known by that name.

Matrices are made also by the electrotype process. In this method the punch of steel and the operation

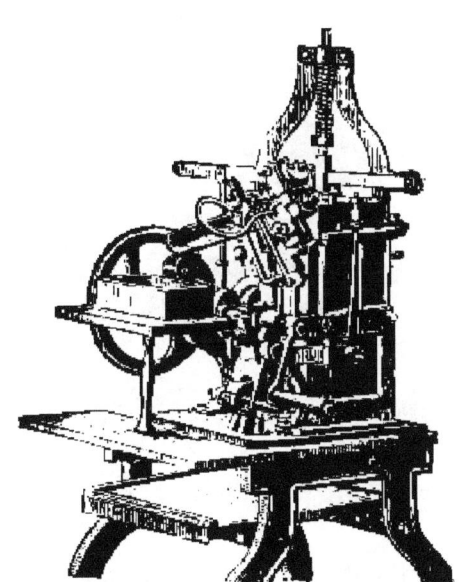

BRUCE HAND TYPE-CASTING MACHINE.

of striking are not required. The characters are first cut on type-metal; after some preparation, the model letters are suspended in the bath of a galvanic battery containing a solution of sulphate of copper. By the action of the electric current on the zinc and copper plates, atoms of copper are liberated, which adhere to the suspended letters. When the deposit has become sufficiently thick, the letters are taken out of the bath and their shells of copper are removed. The shells are then backed up and are fashioned into movable matrices. *The electrotype process of making matrices.*

The Mould consists of two pieces which are counterparts. The interior sides of these two parts, when brought together, are in exact parallel, at a distance which cannot vary. In the upper end of the mould is a seat for the matrix; the lower end is left open for the inflow of the fluid type-metal; between the two ends is the hollow into which the metal flows. The mould is immovable in the direction of the body[1] size of the type, which determines the height of the letter, but can be adjusted to suit the varying widths of different letters. However types may vary in width of face, for any given size of type they must be exactly alike in body. Uniformity of body is secured by having only one mould for all the letters of that body; it is only necessary to change the matrix for each character. Each character requires a separate matrix. *The mould.*

After the mould has been attached to the type-

---

[1] By body is meant the size of a letter considered down a page, at right angles with the printed lines; as, pica body, long-primer body, etc.

casting machine, and the matrix placed in the mould, the process of founding is as follows:

<small>The process of casting type by machinery.</small>

The machine contains a melting-pot to hold the metal, which is kept fluid by a gas-jet or a small furnace. In the centre of the pot is a pump with a plunger. At each revolution of the crank, the plunger forces through an aperture enough of the molten metal to fill the mould and the matrix. The halves of the mould separate; by nicely adjusted leverage the matrix is drawn back from the face of the type, and the type is thrown out. The mould then closes automatically, and the plunger injects a fresh supply of metal, which is dislodged as before in the form of a type. The mould is kept cool either by a blast of cold air or by cold water.

The type comes out with a wedge-shaped strip of metal, called a jet, adhering to its lower end, which is broken off either by automatic breakers or by hand. The body of the type has also a slight shoulder left by the matrix, which is removed by a workman known as the "rubber." The types are then set up in a long row, and are fastened face downwards in a grooved channel. Here the roughness at the jet-fracture is plowed out by a "dresser," with a hand-plane; this leaves the types with a shallow groove between the feet, which enables the body to stand on its feet, thus securing uniformity of height. After other processes of smoothing, the types are examined under a magnifying-glass and every imperfect type is rejected. The perfect types are then packed in paper ready for use. The cast-

TYPE-CASTING AS PRACTISED BY HAND.

ing-machine is operated either by turning a small hand-crank or by steam.

In hand-casting, the workman held in his left hand the mould, which was shielded to protect him from being burned by the molten metal. With a spoon he poured the metal into the mouth-piece of the mould. At the same moment, with a violent jerk, he threw up his left hand, to drive the metal with force against the matrix. This required great dexterity, for if the mould were not thrown up quickly and at the right instant, the metal would not enter the matrix. By this process only about four thousand types could be cast in a day.

<small>Hand-casting.</small>

During the last thirty years, many improvements have been made in automatic type-casting machines. At different times attempts have been made to invent machines which should perform all the processes and deliver types without recourse to manual labor. The most successful of these machines was the one for which Henry Barth was granted a patent in 1888. This machine, automatically, breaks off the jet, plows a groove between the feet, and smooths the feather-edges at the angles. By hand, the average amount cast was 400 in an hour; by the Bruce machine, of ordinary sizes of book-type, the average is 100 in a minute; of small sizes of type, 140 or more can be cast in a minute.

CHAPTER V

SIZES AND STYLES OF TYPES

THE POINT SYSTEM

NO matter how greatly types may differ in width of face, for any given size of type they must be exactly alike in body. The face and the body of a type are cast together at one operation, and while the width of the body varies, according to the width of different letters, such as an *l* or an *m*, the depth of the body, or that part which takes the length of the letter, must always be the same for a given size of type. If there should be the slightest variation in the depth of the body, the form of composed types would not lift

Until recent years there has existed not only a great difference between sizes of type of the same name cast by different foundries, but also a variation between sizes made at different times in the same foundry. To overcome these discrepancies the Point System was adopted, the object of which is to establish a uniform standard for different sizes of type and a uniform gradation of the various sizes. It graduates the sizes by means of a unit of measurement called a "point," which is one-twelfth of the depth of the standard adopted. The standard in the United States is Pica, and the point is therefore about one seventy-second of an inch.

The first practical attempt to secure uniformity of body by a scale of points was made by the noted French type-founder, Pierre Simon Fournier, about the year 1737. After the death of Fournier, some improvements were made in his plan by François Ambroise Didot, the celebrated type-founder of Paris. His classification, however, did not overcome every objection, and for some time, the two systems were used side by side. After some further changes, Didot's system became general in France, and it has been adopted, with modifications, in other parts of Europe. Modern French types are higher than American types, and the two sizes cannot be used together.

In America the first effort to correlate the various bodies was made by George Bruce of New York, in 1822, but his system was not adopted by other American type-founders. After the Chicago fire, Marder, Luse, and Company, whose establishment was entirely burned out, thought the time opportune to readjust all the bodies of type on the new plan. They took for their standard the pica of the MacKellar, Smiths, and Jordan Company, as the one which would be most acceptable to printers and founders, and in 1878 put on sale types made by this system. The Point System was adopted by the American Type-Founders Association in 1886. Although it does not, at present, entirely prevent irregularities, this method of measurement seems likely to prevail throughout the civilized world.

Types used for Text Matter

American Points	Old Names
4	Brilliant
4½	Diamond
5	Pearl
5½	Agate
6	Nonpareil
7	Minion
8	Brevier
9	Bourgeois
10	Long Primer
11	Small Pica
12	Pica
14	English
16	Columbian
18	Great Primer

Among larger sizes are 20-*point*, or *paragon*, 48-*point*, or *canon*, etc. Other sizes are known by the multiples of pica or of sizes above pica, as *double pica, double english, double great primer*, etc. In printing-houses the old names have fallen largely into disuse, and the sizes are spoken of only by their point names.

The sizes most used in books and pamphlets are 12-point (pica), 11-point (small pica), 10-point (long primer), and 8-point (brevier).

The various widths of types receive different names, according to the number of ems to their lower-case alphabets. Type as it usually appears in printed matter has what is called the standard width. As letters progressively decrease in width, they are called lean or condensed, and extra-condensed; as they increase in width, they are known as either fat, broadfaced, expanded, or extended.

Standard Width **Condensed**
Extra Condensed **Extended**

GRADATION OF TYPES

The sizes of types regularly used in book-work range from 4½-point (diamond) to 18-point (great primer), inclusive. Sizes larger than 18-point are seldom employed as text-types.

The following specimen contains twelve sizes of types, in order of gradation, from 18-point to 4½-point, inclusive.

John Gutenberg, a printer of
John Gutenberg, a printer of Mainz, is
John Gutenberg, a printer of Mainz, is re-
John Gutenberg, a printer of Mainz, is regarded
John Gutenberg, a printer of Mainz, is regarded as
John Gutenberg, a printer of Mainz, is regarded as the
John Gutenberg, a printer of Mainz, is regarded as the in-
John Gutenberg, a printer of Mainz, is regarded as the inventor
John Gutenberg, a printer of Mainz, is regarded as the inventor of typog-
John Gutenberg, a printer of Mainz, is regarded as the inventor of typography.
John Gutenberg, a printer of Mainz, is regarded as the inventor of typography. He was a man
John Gutenberg, a printer of Mainz, is regarded as the inventor of typography. He was a man of inventive and

18-point (Great Primer) is used for the text of large quartos and folios and in books for children. The name great primer is probably derived from the early use of the type on a large leaf. From its frequent use in bibles, it received the name of Bible-text[1]. Its French name is *gros romain.*

14-point (English)[2] is not often used as a text-type, except in bibles, prayer-books, and primers. It received the name of English because it was employed by early English printers for their law books, acts of Parliament, and exclusively English works. The Germans call it *Mittel,* as it occupies the middle position among the seven sizes of type most used in printing-offices. The French and the Dutch give it the name of Saint Augustine; from this fact it has been

---

[1] Several fonts of type seem to have taken their names from the works for which they were first used, as bible-text, Saint Augustine, Cicero, brevier, etc

[2] 16-point (Columbian) is not a regular body of book-type and has been seldom employed It was first used as a text-type in 1822, by George Bruce of New York, to supply a size between great primer and english.

inferred that the writings of that father were the first works printed in letters of this size.

12-point (Pica) is the largest size of type commonly used in book-work. It is the standard unit of measurement for bodies of type and widths of furniture, and to divisions of pica all thicknesses of leads are graduated. Pica is employed in works in which it is not necessary to economize space. The French and the Germans give this size the name of Cicero, as the epistles of that writer are said to have been first printed in type of this body.

11-point (Small Pica) is also used in works in which space need not be regarded and in which a handsome appearance is desired. It is employed in octavo volumes, legal reports, and law books.

10-point (Long Primer) is one of the most useful sizes of type. It is a favorite letter for the text of books, many works of fiction being printed in it. It is employed also for the editorials of some newspapers and in poetry. Most of the leading monthly magazines are printed in ten-point Long Primer took its name from its early use in ecclesiastical books.

9-point (Bourgeois) is employed in editorial matter of newspapers, in double-column octavo volumes, and for notes. The name bourgeois suggests a French origin, although type of this body is now known as *Gaillarde* in France. It may have been first employed in small, cheap books printed for the *bourgeoisie*.

8-point (Brevier) takes its name, presumably, from its employment in the breviaries, or Roman Catholic church-books. It is used for the body of daily newspapers, as the text-type of some magazines, for notes and extracts, and in cheap editions of literature. It is often employed as the text-type of large works in which space must be economized. The Germans give this type the names of *Petit*, and *Jungfer* (maiden letter), because of its comeliness.

7-point (Minion) is employed chiefly for newspapers. It is used also for notes and indexes in book-work, and in large dictionaries and encyclopedias. The name minion may have been given to it to indicate not only that it was the smallest letter in use at the time of its introduction, but that it was regarded as a darling of a type

6-point (Nonpareil) is used on newspapers, for tabular work, and for notes and indexes in small volumes It is the smallest type that should appear in book-work, as types more diminutive cannot be read for any length of time without injury to the eyes. It must have been regarded as a marvel of skill and as the smallest letter that could be cut, as it has retained the same name in all countries.

5½-point (Agate) is employed for advertisements and market reports in newspapers, and for printing in which compression is necessary. It is used for pocket-bibles and prayer-books In England it is known as Ruby.

5 point (Pearl) is used for pocket bibles, prayer-books, pocket-dictionaries, and side and cut-in notes and references It is the smallest type of any practical use.

4½-point (Diamond) is the smallest type regularly cast by founders and is seldom used. Bibles and prayer-books are occasionally printed in letters of this body

4-point (Brilliant), is scarcely more than a curiosity, although miniature volumes have been printed in it. When seen through a magnifying glass, it is as distinct and beautiful as types of larger body. It is a product of the nineteenth century.

3-point (Excelsior), a size still smaller than brilliant, is used in America for music, piece-fractions, and borders.

A letter has been produced still smaller than excelsior. Henri Didot, of the family of celebrated French type-founders, in 1827, when sixty-six years old, cut a font of type on the body of 2½ points by the Didot system, each letter being clear and distinct; to this size he gave the name of *microscopique*. Twenty-five lines of this letter would about cover the space of one American inch.

Styles of Types

Although many styles of types have been issued by the various foundries, the different series are mainly combinations or variations of the following:

Roman
Italic

Black Letter
- 𝕺𝖑𝖉 𝕰𝖓𝖌𝖑𝖎𝖘𝖍
- German Text
- Church Text
- Tudor

Script
Antique
Title-type
Elzevir old style

CLARENDON
GOTHIC
DORIC
RUNIC
𝔐𝔦𝔰𝔰𝔞𝔩
BOLD FACE
THIN FACE

CHAPTER VI

TYPESETTING

Typesetting by hand. AS the hand-compositor works he has before him two inclined cases, one above the other, called, respectively, Upper Case and Lower Case. These contain the types—the upper case, capitals and small capitals, and the lower case, small letters. The compositor selects the proper types and forms with them a line in an instrument held in his left hand, known as the composing-stick. This "stick" is really a three-sided tray or box; for ordinary book and newspaper work, it is from six to eight inches long. The width of the matter composed, or the length of the line, is regulated by a sliding piece of metal and a screw. The line is "justified," or made the proper length, by the insertion and rearrangement of spaces, or pieces of metal of standard widths, which separate one word from another. After the stick has been filled, the matter set up is placed on a shallow frame or pan, called a galley. When no greater spacing is desired between the lines than the types themselves afford, the matter is said to be "solid." When wider spacing is desired, thin strips of metal, called leads, are inserted between the lines; the work is then known as "leaded." The composed types are made into pages, and are locked up in forms on the imposing stone.

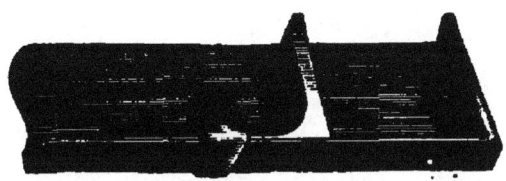

COMPOSING STICK.

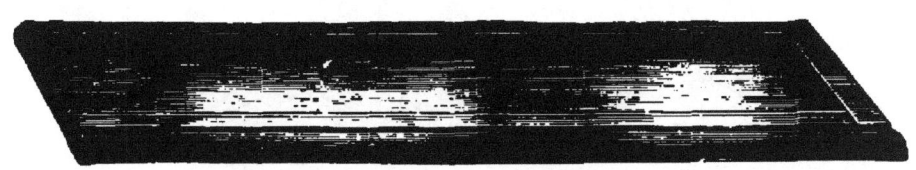

GALLEY.

Until 1821 no attempt was made to set type by machinery, and even then the effort was only theoretical. About 1822 Dr. William Church, a native of the United States, while endeavoring to bring out other inventions in England, announced that he had discovered a method of casting and composing type automatically at an unusual speed; his method, however, did not include distribution. He was granted a patent in England, but it seems that nothing more than a wooden model of his machine was ever made. In America the first patents were granted in 1840 and 1841 to Frederick Rosenberg and to Young and Delcambre. The first typesetting machine which continued to be used for practical work for a number of years was the one invented by William H. Mitchel, a brother of the Irish patriot. He took out his first patent in 1853, but his machine was finally superseded by others, for want of a good distributer.

The Alden machine was built in 1857, but was not continued in commercial use. The Burr-Kastenbein machine, requiring hand-justification, came out in the 70's; the Thorne, also requiring justification by hand, was invented about 1880. These were the only machines successfully used in the United States until 1886, when the Linotype was introduced. The Mergenthaler, or Linotype, is the typesetting machine generally employed in this country; among other machines are the Simplex, the Burr-Kastenbein or Empire, and the Lanston. Among the machines brought out in Great Britain were the Frazer, the Hattersley, and the Mackie.

Probably the first attempt to produce a machine to set ordinary types and justify them automatically was made by Felt, who was granted a patent in 1867. The machine failed to operate successfully. The first successful machine to set, justify, and distribute type automatically was the Paige, completed about 1890. This machine is not in the market because of its great expense.

Simplest form of typesetting machine. The typesetting machine in its simplest form merely sets the type supplied by the founders; spacing out, justifying, making-up, and distributing must all be done by hand or on other machines. In the simple form of machine about eighty-four characters are employed. The types of each character are placed in a narrow channel of brass, about two feet long, side by side, and in a vertical position, before the compositor. The machine is operated in the same manner as a typewriter: when the compositor strikes a certain letter on the keyboard, the corresponding character falls in position. This machine can only *set* types in a continuous line; another operator is required to justify the types, or to make them up in lines of uniform length. The McMillan machine has a mated justifying apparatus, but the distributer is a distinct machine.

All the simpler forms of typesetting machines have been generally superseded by those in which composition, casting, and distribution are combined in one machine.

The Lanston machine. The Lanston machine, which went into commercial use about 1899, both casts and sets individual

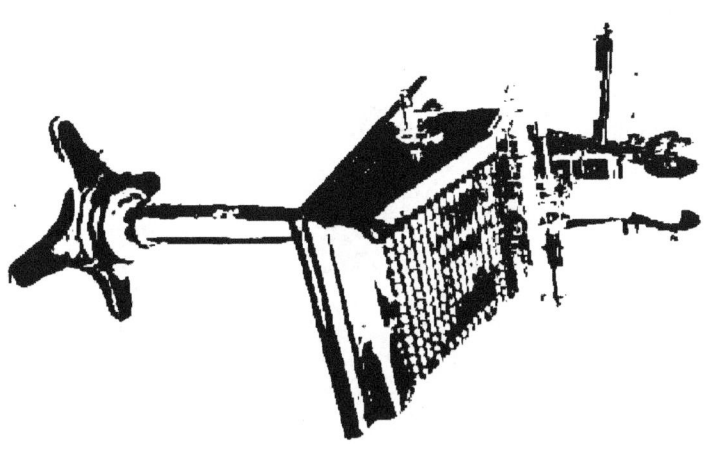

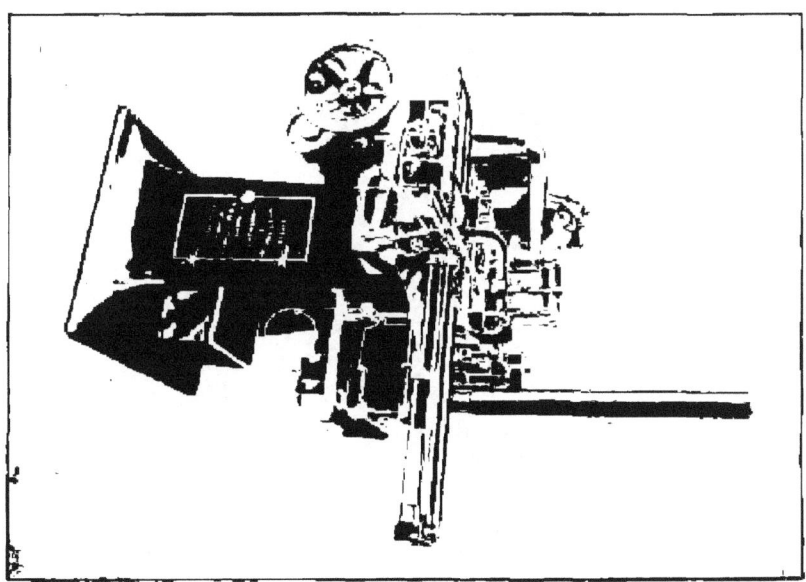

type. It permits the free and equal use of all the upper and lower case characters; these it casts and composes in justified lines by a single automatic operation, which is controlled by a perforated paper ribbon, the product of the manual operation of the keyboard. The composed matter has the same appearance as hand-work; the types, however, are always new, and the lines are more evenly justified. Corrections are made at a case of sorts, by the withdrawal of the wrong character and the insertion of the right one. The Lanston machine is preferred by some authors for book-work, because it permits the correction of errors without discarding the whole line. This typesetting machine is in use in a large number of printing-offices, and it is claimed that it furnishes a letterpress equal to that of the best foundry type.

The Mergenthaler, or Linotype, casts the letters properly justified, with spaces between words, in solid bars of the length of line desired. The compositor dislodges brass matrices instead of types, and also space-bands. The latter are wedge-shaped, and are released, one by one, at the end of each word. The wedges are about three inches long; the thin part only at first is inserted, but just before the bar is cast, an apparatus is released which drives the whole series of letters and space-bands to just the right pressure required to produce the even justification of the line.

The Mergenthaler machine, or Linotype.

The matrices are then carried in front of the mould. The mould passes before the pot containing the molten metal, which is ejected through a row of holes into the mould. The metal chills and solidifies immediately, and the casting is accomplished without delaying the work of the operator. The cast line, or *linotype*, passes between knives to be finished to exact size, and is then placed on the galley. The matrices are at once returned to their channels in the magazine, and the space-bands slide back into their box ready for immediate use.

During composition on the Linotype, corrections can be made by changing or transposing any matrix in a line. If a correction is desired after the bar is cast, the whole line must be reset. The discarded bar is thrown into the melting-pot; the linotypes are also remelted after they have served their purpose. In operating the machine, as soon as one line is finished, the compositor starts another line; all that he is required to do is to manipulate the keys and start the lines.

The present Linotype is the result of experiments begun in 1876. In a crude form it was developed about 1883, and was put into commercial use in 1886. It is employed in about thirteen hundred offices in America, including both large and small newspapers and many book-houses, such as Harper and Brothers and D. Appleton and Company. The Mergenthaler machine is used also by most of the leading newspapers of Great Britain, quite extensively in Germany and France, and indeed, to some extent, in almost every part of the world. In the Boston Public Library, where the Linotype is employed to produce

MERGENTHALER TYPESETTING MACHINE (LINOTYPE).

card catalogues, etc., twenty-three languages are printed.

Typesetting machines are employed chiefly for newspaper printing and for work which must be done quickly; many publishers also use them. In quality, the product of the machine is not equal to handwork, although in some instances only an experienced eye could detect the difference. The machine reduces the cost of composition—one of the simpler forms setting types three or four times as fast as can be done by hand, and the output of the Mergenthaler being six or eight times greater than that of the hand-compositor. It is only by employing the Linotype, which has so greatly cheapened typesetting, that our newspapers can afford to furnish to the public the vast amount of reading matter which is received daily.

Measurement of Type Matter

The amount of matter composed is estimated by *ems*, or the square of the body of the font of type used, to which the letter *m* comes nearest in size of all the lower case letters. The compositor is paid for the number of ems contained in any piece of work he sets. The smaller the type, the greater, of course, will be the number of ems in a page. There will be about the same number of ems in the complete copy, whether it is set in large or small type; so that the cost of composition will be about the same in either case, although in small type the number of pages will be less.

The space that can be covered by one thousand em quadrats must be paid for as one thousand ems, whether the matter is leaded or solid. The actual number of pieces of metal in the space is not considered. When type is mixed, each size is estimated by itself.

Leading

When we consider that printing of a rudimentary kind had existed for so many centuries, and that during the whole of the early part of the fifteenth century examples with words or even whole lines of inscriptions were being produced, we can only wonder that the discovery of printing from movable types should have been made so late. It has been said that inventions will always be made when the need for them has arisen, and this is the real reason, perhaps, why the discovery of printing was delayed. —E. Gordon Duff: *Early Printed Books*

The method adopted by the earliest printers to obtain impressions from their blocks was to lay the sheet to be printed on the already inked block, and to rub it carefully. Wood-engravers of the present day take proofs in the same manner. The plan was continued for block-printing many years after the invention of movable types. Mr. Ottley, however, describes several of the earliest wood-blocks, which he had no doubt were printed by means of a press.— William Blades: *The Biography and Typography of William Caxton.*

The decree of Star Chamber in 1637, which limited the number of English printers, did not check the growth of printing more effectually than the stamp duty of four pence levied in 1815 on every English newspaper. Printers everywhere had to encounter disabilities made by society as well as by law. Even in America, Franklin's brother was practically boycotted in Boston, Bradford had to leave Philadelphia for New York, and Zenger of New York had to stand trial for criminal libel in making proper comment. At an earlier date Governor Berkeley of Virginia thanked God that there were no printers in that colony, and hoped that there would be none. Printers [at the beginning of the nineteenth century] had to be content with conditions as they were. They had little inducement to improve their workmanship or to extend their field of activity.—THEODORE L. DE VINNE, in New York *Evening Post*, "Printing in the Nineteenth Century."

When still wider spacing is employed, the work is called "triple-leaded."

CHAPTER VII

JOB-WORK

ALL the miscellaneous work of a printing-office, beyond book and newspaper work, is included in the general term, Job-work. It comprises:

Placards, posters, hand-bills, pamphlets, circulars, invitations, programs, cards and tickets of all kinds, bills of fare, blank forms, bills, checks, receipts, certificates, labels, letter-heads, note-heads, printed envelopes, account-book headings, order-books, monthly statements, and other miscellaneous matter of like nature.

In ordering job-printing, as in all other business transactions, there should be a definite understanding of just what is wanted. The dimensions of the work should be specified, also the size and style of type desired, and the words or lines to be given greatest prominence. Extracts and foot-notes are always put in smaller type than the body of the work; for this reason, they should be carefully distinguished from the text. Resetting matter means delay in the work and additional expense to the person ordering. The kind of paper desired should be stated. Samples of paper, from which a selection can be made, will always be cheerfully furnished by the printer.

For even such small work as a card or the printing on an envelope, it insures satisfactory results to see a proof. In rush work this is not always practicable, and the judgment and taste of the printer must be depended upon; but a glance at a proof would prevent many flagrant errors in spelling, etc., often seen in announcements, and would save the person who pays for the work vexation and disappointment.

Regard should be had to the style of type and the paper suitable for the subject. It will be clear to every one that a light fancy type is unsuitable for a serious subject; neither should the same kind of paper or card be used for a business announcement as for a musical program or an invitation to a reception or a dance. Harmony should be observed also between the type and the paper. A thin-face type does not always show well on rough paper, nor does black letter look best on a smooth surface. *General appearance.*

Narrow margins around printed matter, whether it be a card, a circular, or the page of a book, detract from the elegance of its appearance. When the text is leaded, that is when there is spacing between the lines, it is more easily read than when printed solid. Leading, however, is not always possible when matter must be compressed into a small space.

A long narrow page should be avoided. The proportion of 5 to $7\frac{1}{2}$, for some work, is pleasing in appearance. For a page of an oblong shape, Bigelow gives as a rule that the diagonal from the folio in the upper corner to the opposite lower corner should be just twice the width of the text; in a quarto, or square page, the proportion of the diagonal to the width should be $10\frac{1}{2} : 6\frac{1}{4}$. These rules have been established in conformity to a law of proportion which completely satisfies the eye.

Title-pages, headings, cards, etc.

In title-pages, headings, cards, etc., a due proportion should be observed in the prominence of the lines, so as to show, as nearly as possible, the relation of one line to another. It has heretofore been the custom to contrast the lines in length, weight, size, face, etc., the most important line being put the largest, and sometimes the blackest, type, the gradation being followed down to the least important line. At present, such matter is frequently set entirely in one style of type of different sizes, the most important line, of course, taking the largest letters. Some of the new roman and shaded types thus used for cards and announcements produce an especially pleasing effect, as they give the work something of the elegance of engraving.

The type of the main line should be in proportion to the size of the page or card, for if it is too large it offends the eye. If a line rather unimportant is set in letters too large or in type too distinctive, it jars upon one's sense of artistic harmony. The principal line should never be placed at the very top of a card or page, and printers do not begin a main line with words of little value, such as "a," "the," etc. A very long line can sometimes be broken, and one half placed below, a little to the right; but in such divisions, regard must be had to the general effect of the lines in combination with others. Several short lines in succession at the top of a circular or card produce a pyramidal effect and should be avoided. Too much matter on a title-page spoils its appearance.

When the compositor is allowed to transpose the wording, the appearance of the work can frequently be greatly improved.

In job-work, words may be made emphatic in several ways: they may be set in lines by themselves; large or distinctive types may be used; they may be underlined; the white spaces may be varied, etc., etc. Care should be taken not to give emphasis to too many words or lines, as the most important ideas thereby lose their significance.

CHAPTER VIII

PAPER

AT first, paper, both ancient and modern, was made entirely by hand. In 1799 a paper-machine was invented by Louis Robert, a clerk employed by the Messrs. Didot of the celebrated Essonnes paper-mills near Paris, and this caused a great development of the industry. The manufacture was introduced into England, through the agency of the Messrs. Fourdrinier, and the first paper-machine in that country was erected in 1804 at Frogmoor Mill, near Boxmoor, Herts. Henry and Sealy Fourdrinier, of London, bought the English patents, and so perfected the machine that it has since been given the name of Fourdrinier. In America the first steam paper-mill was started at Pittsburg, in 1816. The first cylinder machine for the manufacture of paper was designed by Thomas Gilpin, and was employed by him in 1817, in his mills on the Brandywine. Since about 1820 paper made by machinery has supplanted hand-made paper, except fine grades used for special purposes.

The staples, or the materials, from which writing and printing papers are made are wood-pulp, rags and esparto.[1] The staple of wrapping-paper is old

---
[1] Esparto is the name of two or three species of grass found in Southern Europe and Northern Africa.

ropes and jute. The finest writing and printing papers, whether made by hand or machinery, are manufactured from linen and cotton rags. A great part of paper-making material is a by-product obtained from the refuse of other manufactures, such as waste paper, rags, old rope, old bagging, etc. At the present day paper is put to so many uses that rags cannot be obtained in sufficient quantities, and the greater amount of even white paper is now made from wood-fibre. Paper can be made of almost any vegetable fibre, but those fibres are strongest which are most completely interlaced. The woods generally used are the poplar, pine, spruce, and hemlock.

The idea of making paper from wood-pulp arose in the early part of the nineteenth century. Various patents were granted, but it was not until about 1855 that wood began to take the place of rags for book and newspaper work. A distinction must be made between wood-pulp and wood-fibre: the pulp is produced by mechanical means, or by grinding; the fibre by chemical treatment, or by a process which separates from the wood all resinous and gummy substances, and leaves what is called *cellulose*, or fibre divested of all incrusting matter. Wood-pulp generally receives an admixture of wood-fibre to give it strength. Wood-pulp and wood-fibre.

The manufacture of paper really begins with the first step required to prepare the stock. In making wood-pulp, the bark and knots are first separated from the wood. The wood is then cut into convenient lengths and is put into a machine, termed a wood- Preparation of the stock.

pulp grinder, which tears off the fibres. To produce wood, or chemical, fibre, the wood is cut into chips, dusted, and is then boiled in an alkaline or acid solution, in a vessel known as a digester. The chemicals separate the gummy or resinous substances from the fibre, which, when washed and bleached, is almost pure cellulose. It is soft and of considerable strength.

Esparto, or Spanish grass, is cleaned and sorted by hand, and is afterward boiled in an alkaline solution. Jute, hemp, and waste matter are all treated in about the same way, being boiled in alkaline solutions. Cotton and linen rags are passed first through threshers, then through cutters, and are afterward boiled in a solution of caustic soda.

After the preparation of the staple, the making of it into pulp and the manufacture of the pulp into paper are about the same whether rags or other varieties of stock are employed. The process of the preparation of the pulp, whether for machine or for hand-made paper, is substantially the same, but in making paper by machinery each operation is performed on a much larger scale.

Paper-making by machinery. In making paper by machinery, the rags are first put into a thresher or dusting-machine. After they have passed through this, women sort them by hand, and remove all extraneous substances, such as buttons, hooks and eyes, bone, india-rubber, leather, and pieces of metal, at the same time loosening all hems and knots. The rags are then cut into small pieces, either by hand or machinery; for the common qualities of paper, machine-cutting is used. When the rags are cut by hand, the sorter stands at a long table, to which scythe-blades are attached; the back of the blade is towards the sorter, who draws the cloth against the edge. The rags are again dusted and sent to openings in the floor of the room, underneath which are brought the mouths of large boilers called rotaries. The boilers contain a solution of soda ash, caustic soda, or lime in water. The mouths of the rotaries are closed, steam is introduced, and the rags are boiled under pressure for several hours; by this treatment all fatty, glutinous, or coloring substances are separated from the pure fibre. Afterwards, the rags are drained and taken to the washing-and-beating engines. They are sometimes washed in one engine and beaten in another, sometimes both operations are performed in the same machine. This engine is an oblong shallow tub or vat. The rags are placed in it, with a sufficient quantity of water, and are brought by power under the action of two sets of knives, by which they are subdivided. The water in the washing cylinder is constantly changing, affording a continual supply of fresh water and the carrying off of the dirty fluid. The rags are thus treated from three to five hours, at the end of which time they are sufficiently cleaned. They are now known as *half-stuff*.

The next step is bleaching. A solution of chloride of lime and some sulphuric acid are added to the half-stuff, which is emptied into a chest or drainer. Here the bleaching is finished. The pulp is then washed to free it from the chemical products adhering to it, and for this purpose it is again put into the engine or tub, the roller with knives being raised to avoid cutting the fibre. The stock is now beaten to the desired fineness and is sent to the stuff-chest. This completes the preparation of the pulp for actual paper-making.

From the stuff-chest the pulp is pumped into a regulating-box, or supply-box. The stuff is sent to the Fourdrinier machine through a pipe containing a rapidly flowing stream of water. After passing through the preliminary parts of the machine, the pulp is deposited upon a wire-cloth, which is a huge belt, having both a forward and a lateral motion. The pulp is laid upon this belt evenly, and is still in a liquid condition; the water oozes out through the bottom into a depression below. The constant vibration of the wire-cloth, by means of a shake attachment, throws some of the fibres across the machine, while the motion or travel of the belt causes the lay of the fibre in the other direction. Endless rubber-bands, called deckles, extend on each side on top of the wire; these prevent the pulp from spreading beyond the edges of the wire, and also determine the width of the paper. The deckles continue about two-thirds of the distance of the run of the belt, by which time the paper is formed, but is still in a pulpy condition. A cylindrical frame covered with wire-cloth, known as the dandy-roll, passes over the pulpy paper and presses the fibres more closely together. Upon the dandy-roll are frequently placed letters, monograms, or other signs, which may be seen in the finished paper when held up to the light. To produce these marks in the paper, some of the wires are made to project a little more than usual, or other wires are fastened over them, the paper thereby being made thinner in such places. These letters or signs are produced also by depressing the wires where a mark is desired, thus causing the paper in those places to be thicker.

The web then passes over the suction-boxes, and just as it leaves the wire-cloth it passes under the couch-rolls, after which moisture is expelled by two sets of rollers. The remaining moisture is driven out by heat. Thus far, no heat has been employed.

The paper is now sent to the driers, a series of iron cylinders of large diameter, heated by steam. Accompanied by a felt or belt of duck, it passes over and under these cylinders, becoming drier and more compact as it approaches the end of the machine. The web then passes into a tub of animal sizing. If the paper is to be "loft-dried," it is cut into sheets and taken to the loft, where it is hung on poles. The cheaper varieties remain there two days, the finer grades a week. "Machine-dried" paper passes from the size-tub into a mechanical drier, without being cut into sheets. *The driers.*

The Fourdrinier machine, above described, has been improved in all its details, but in theory its construction is about the same as when invented by Robert. This machine was first employed in the United States about 1827, at Springfield, Massachusetts. *The Fourdrinier machine.*

52 PAPER

The Cylinder machine. On the Cylinder machine no lateral motion is given to the wire-cloth; the paper therefore felts in but one direction. Paper made on the Cylinder machine is stronger in the direction of its length than that made by the Fourdrinier machine, but is weaker in its breadth. The cylinder machine is used in the United States for the manufacture of hanging-papers, wrapping-papers, and straw and binders' boards.

The calenders. To receive a finish, all papers pass through a "stack" of calenders, which consists of a series of polished iron rollers, mounted one above the other. Paper which goes but once through the calenders is given the name of "machine-finish." Loft-dried paper is calendered in single sheets; machine-dried, in the roll.

The supercalenders. To supercalender paper, it is passed between a series of rollers called supercalenders; some of these are made of chilled iron, others of sheets of paper or of compressed disks of cotton.

Sizing. Sizing is given to paper for the purpose of removing its porous and absorbent character, so that when written upon the ink will not spread. Vegetable sizing is put into the engines; animal sizing is given on the machine, by passing the web through a trough containing a solution of gelatine.

Loading. To fill up the pores or interstices, paper is loaded with some other substance. This not only gives the paper a finer surface but also makes it heavier. Kaolin or china clay is the loading material for ordinary paper; for the finer grades, sulphate of lime or pearl hardening is used. The clay is made into a

STACK OF 52-INCH SUPERCALENDERS—FRONT VIEW.

thin cream and is put into the pulp while the latter is in the beating-engine.

When paper first comes from the machine, little ridges or hollows are found on its surface, resembling those on the rind of an orange. To make the paper smoother, it is surface-coated, and the most delicate half-tones can then be printed upon it. In surfaced papers the mixture is applied by brushes, and the paper is calendered by steel rollers to the degree of finish desired. The oftener the paper passes through the rollers, the higher will be the finish. Some papers are brushed to a finish instead of being put through the rollers. *Surface-coating.*

It is not possible to make from the raw materials absolutely white paper, as the web always inclines either to blue or yellow. Paper is therefore shaded slightly towards a buff or bluish tint. This is generally accomplished by putting a coloring substance, which dissolves very slowly, into the pulp in the engine. *Shading.*

As has been stated above, the preparation of the pulp, whether for hand- or machine-made paper, is substantially the same. The old stamps or beaters have been superseded by the Hollander or beating engine, which is still in use. In making paper by hand, the pulp is carried to the working-vat, a vessel either of wood or stone, about five feet square and four feet deep, with a flaring top. In the vat the pulp is mixed with water and is heated by means of a steam-pipe. The mould for making the paper is a wooden frame, with bars about an inch and a half apart, flush with *Paper-making by hand.*

one edge of the frame. Parallel wires, about fifteen or twenty to the inch, are laid upon these bars, lengthwise of the frame. A movable frame, called a deckle, fits upon the mould, the two forming a shallow tray, with a wire bottom like a sieve. Paper made in such a mould is known as "wove" paper.

Wove paper.

When small wires placed close together, with coarser wires running across them at equidistant intervals, form the bottom of the mould, in place of the wire-cloth used as the bottom for wove paper, the paper made in such a mould takes the impression of all these wires. It is then given the name of "laid" paper.

Laid paper.

The mould or wire-frame on which the pulp is formed is raised where the water-mark, or trademark, is desired. The sheet in that part is thereby made thinner than in other places, and the design remains impressed in each sheet.

The watermark.

The workman dips the mould into the vat containing the fluid pulp, and takes up a sufficient quantity to form a sheet of paper. Great dexterity is needed to make a perfect sheet, and to follow this with other perfect sheets all of even weight; this depends on the skill of eye and hand acquired by experience. The vatman gives the mould an oscillating motion, to cause the intermixture of the fibres necessary to secure uniformity of texture. Gradually the water drains through, the pulp solidifies and assumes a peculiar shiny appearance, which indicates the completion of the first step of the process. The deckle is then taken off, and the mould is sent to a workman known as the "coucher," who deposits the sheet upon a piece of felt. Another piece of felt is placed upon the paper, and this process is continued until the pile contains six or eight quires. The pile is then subjected to great pressure. A workman known as a "layer" separates the pieces of felt and the paper. The sheets are again pressed to remove, so far as possible, the felt-marks and the moisture, and are then hung in a loft to dry. When dry, the paper is sized. Sizing is made of some material containing a great deal of gelatine, such as sheeps' feet, or pieces of skin cut off by curriers before the hides are tanned. These materials are boiled to a jelly and strained, and a small quantity of alum is added. The sheets are spread out in a tub containing the sizing diluted with water. Care is taken that the sheets shall be equally moistened. After sizing, the paper is again pressed and slowly dried. Women take out the knots and imperfections with small knives, and separate the perfect from the imperfect sheets. After being again pressed, the paper is counted into reams. These reams when pressed and tied up are ready to be sent to the warehouse. There is but one mill in the United States which produces hand-made paper, that of the L. L. Brown Paper Company at Adams, Massachusetts. In the vat-mills of Europe, after the preparation of the pulp by machinery, paper is made by hand in about the same way as in this country. In some towns, however, the same process has been employed for several centuries. In a number of the ancient mills at Amalfi, Italy, the rags are still beaten by hammers.

Deckle-edged papers.

Deckle-edge is the name given to papers which are rough on the outer edges. In making paper by hand, the pulp is shaken in a sieve, and the sides, consequently, are uneven. When paper first issues from the machine, it is rough on the outer edges, next to the deckles, and is afterwards trimmed. Deckle-edged machine paper, however, can be made in narrow strips of any desired width. This is done by putting in a number of deckle-straps on the wire-cloth, so as to give the true deckle. The edge thus formed is more feathery than that of regular hand-made paper; it occurs on two sides instead of four.

Classes of paper.

Paper may be divided into four general classes: Printing-paper (book and newspaper), Writing-paper, Wrapping- or Packing-paper, and special or miscellaneous papers.

Printing-papers.

Machine-finish.—A paper with an unglazed surface, having passed but once through the calenders.

Wove.—A paper which receives no other impression than that made by the weave of the wire-cloth and the dandy-roll.

Laid.—When made by hand, a paper which takes the impression of both the small and the coarse wires which form the bottom of the mould. In machine-made paper, the equidistant parallel lines are produced by a series of wires which pass around the exterior of the dandy-roll.

Calendered.—A paper which receives a surface by being passed through a series of polished iron rollers, known as calenders. This operation makes the paper even and also gives it a gloss.

Supercalendered.—A paper which receives a still higher finish than calendered paper, by being subjected to the action of supercalenders, which are a series of rollers, some made of chilled iron, others of sheets of paper or of compressed disks of cotton.

Coated.—A paper which has received a coating of white material, such as china clay, or gypsum, sulphate of barytes, etc.

Coated and supercalendered papers are used for first-class magazines and illustrated books, as they take the impression of a plate better than many other papers.

Enameled papers are coated with a colored substance which adds both to their weight and thickness. They are used for covers.

Deckle-edge.—Deckle-edged papers are rough on the outer edge. They are made both by hand and by machinery.

Plate paper.—Paper which has passed between highly polished metal plates or heavy rollers which give a powerful pressure. Plate paper is a high grade of book stock, and has the same finish on both sides. It takes well the impression of printers' ink, and receives the most delicate lines of half-tones.

Copperplate paper is unsized paper, unfinished on one side and calendered on the other.

India.—A thin soft paper, of a pale yellow tint, used for taking the first and choicest impressions of engravings. The impressions are known as India proofs. As India paper is too thin to bear handling, it is mounted on vellum. The sheets are kept in a dry place and can be preserved for years.

Writing-paper has a smooth surface, as it is made with a sizing or glue. Without the sizing, the ink would penetrate the paper and render each line of the writing too thick. Writing-paper sometimes has the same name, but not always the same size, as printing-papers.

Among writing-papers are:

Bond.—A fine stock of paper, usually uncalendered and very strong.

Linen.—A paper made from the same stock as a bond paper, but laid, and usually of a rougher finish.

Ledger.—The finest qualities of writing-paper large in size. Ledger-paper is very strong and has good erasing qualities.

The fine varieties of writing-papers are, of course, made from linen rags.

Some of the special papers are used just as they come from the mill; others are prepared for special purposes by manufacturers known as converters. These products may be divided broadly into special papers and converted papers. Among special papers may be mentioned blotting, copying, India, Japan, manifold, parchment, rice, sand, safety, silver, sponge, and tracing paper; among converted papers are carbolic acid, carbon, emery, glass, gold or gilt, oiled, photographic, satin, silver, and test paper. Coated paper, safety paper, and tracing paper are sometimes subjected to treatment by converters. India, Japan, parchment, and safety papers are used also for printing purposes.

Sizes of Paper

At the present day paper is made of almost any size, to suit the needs or the taste of the publisher or author. Although each of the various sizes has received a special name, but few of these names are in common use; in giving an order for paper, it is customary to designate the size in inches.

The standard sizes of paper made in America are the following:

OOK PAPERS

22 x 28 inches.	28 x 42 inches.
24 x 38 "	32 x 44 "
25 x 38 "	36 x 48 "
26 x 40 "	

WRITING PAPERS

	Inches		Inches.
Cap	14 x 17	Double Medium	18 x 46
Double Cap	17 x 28	Royal	19 x 24
Crown	15 x 19	Double Royal	24 x 38
Double Crown	19 x 30	Double Royal	19 x 48
Demy	16 x 21	Super Royal	20 x 28
Double Demy	21 x 32	Imperial	23 x 31
Double Demy	16 x 42	Elephant	23 x 28
Folio	17 x 22	Columbier	23 x 34
Double Folio	22 x 34	Atlas	26 x 33
Medium	18 x 23	Double Elephant	27 x 40
Double Medium	23 x 36	Antiquarian	31 x 53

Folio is more used than any other size of writing-paper. Paper, as a rule, nowadays, runs 500 sheets to the ream.

FOLDING THE SHEETS FOR BINDING

For book and magazine work,[1] paper is usually sent from the manufacturer to the printing-house in flat sheets, and on the flat-bed press, which is generally employed for this class of work, it is printed in flat sheets. The flat sheets are sent to the bindery, and, as a rule, are folded by machinery. Some magazines are folded on the press on which they are printed.

A flat sheet folded once gives two leaves or four pages, which is called *folio*. Halving the long side of a flat sheet gives *broad folio;* halving the short side gives *long folio*.

Halving the length of the two sides of broad folio gives four leaves or eight pages, or *quarto*.

Quarto folded once gives eight leaves or sixteen pages, or *octavo*. By continuing the folding, we obtain 16mo, 32mo, 64mo, etc. *Mo* or ° means the number of *leaves* to the sheet, or the number of *pages* on *one* side of the sheet.

The terms *octavo, quarto, folio*, etc., *do not indicate the size of the leaf,* but merely denote the number of leaves into which a sheet has been folded. When sheets of paper were made in but few sizes, octavo, quarto, or folio, as applied to books, denoted a volume of a certain size; now that sheets may be made of almost any size, these terms no longer indicate fixed dimensions. A book may be folio, it may be large folio, or it may be small folio. The size of the leaf is indicated by the name or the

---

[1] For newspapers, which are printed on rotary presses, paper is used in the web or roll. The rotary or web press is used also, to some extent, in the production of books and magazines, for which, of course, the paper must be furnished in the roll.

size of the sheet from which the leaf is taken; as, cap, crown, demy, folio, medium, royal, etc.

The following diagrams show the usual forms for folding, but for special purposes other methods are sometimes employed.

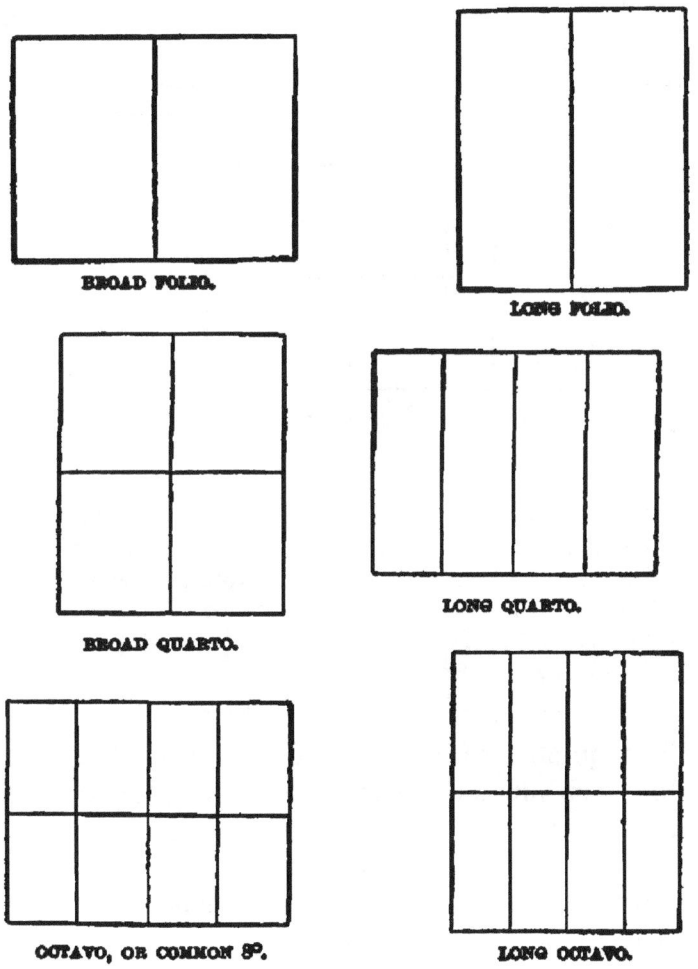

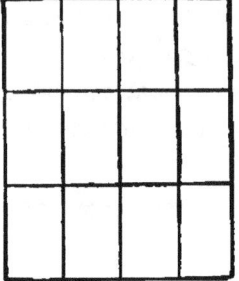
DUODECIMO, OR 12°

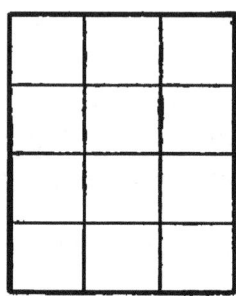
SQUARE 12°

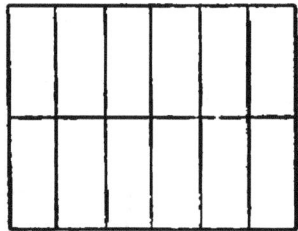
LONG 12°

Table

Flat sheet		1 leaf or 2 pages
1 fold	folio........	2 leaves or 4 pages
2 folds........	quarto......	4 leaves or 8 pages
3 folds	octavo......	8 leaves or 16 pages
4 folds	16mo	16 leaves or 32 pages
5 folds........	32mo	32 leaves or 64 pages
6 folds........	64mo	64 leaves or 128 pages.

The number of leaves in each case, in the above table, is obtained by folding right across the previous fold.

More than four folds are seldom given to a sheet, as the constant doubling of the paper causes the leaves to be of unequal size.

PAPER

It has been the practice to print 12° with twenty-four pages to the sheet, and then cut off eight pages and fold them in as an inset. Presses are now made large enough, however, to print thirty-two, sixty-four, or even a greater number of pages at a time. 24° is simply 12° doubled.

By printing part of the sheet as an inset, a printer can often use, without waste, a certain size of paper on work for which the regular methods of imposing pages would not enable the paper to be employed to advantage.

Thirds, sixes, and eighteens are no longer used in book-work. With the least possible handling of the sheets, the greater will be the economy, and presses are now so built that a large number of pages can be printed at once. The sheets are afterwards cut into sections, each containing the number of pages desired.

The following size notation has been adopted by the American Library Association:

FOLD SYMBOL Never use for size	SIZE LETTER Never use for fold	OUTSIDE HEIGHT In centimetres
48°	Fe	Up to 10
32°	Tt	10 to 12.5
24°	T	12.5 to 15
16°	S	15 to 17.5
12°	D	17.5 to 20
8°	O	20 to 25
4°	Q	25 to 30
f°	F	30 to 35
	F⁴	35 to 40
	F⁵	40 to 50
	F⁶	50 to 60

SIGNATURES

A signature is a figure or letter placed at the bottom of the first page of each sheet of a volume, to indicate the place the sheet should have in the completed book. The name signature is given also to the sheet bearing this figure or letter; thus, we say that a work is printed in twenty-four signatures, which means twenty-four sections.[1] The figure or letter should be placed on the first page of each sheet or section of the book, under the text, to the left of the page. In America numerical signatures are generally employed.

Signatures serve several purposes:

1. They designate the pages of which a sheet is composed. If we refer to a certain sheet and call it signature 3, we know exactly which pages of the book it contains.

2. They serve as an aid to the binder in gathering the sheets together, so that they fall in proper order; they assist also in collating, that is, in verifying the gathering. If the letters follow in due alphabetical order, the sheets must be in their right positions.

Signatures were used by the scribes long before the invention of printing. At first, these marks were placed on the extreme edge of the printed

---

[1] A section of a book is the number of leaves which are sewed together at once. A small sheet may make a section, but large sheets on which are printed thirty-two, sixty-four, or a greater number of pages, are cut into two, four, or eight sections, according to the way the book is made up. A sheet is always at least one section, but a section is not always a sheet.

sheet, so that they might be cut off by the knife of the binder. In some old books they may still be seen half cut off. It was thought that this method improved the appearance of the page.

MAKE-UP OF A BOOK

The order observed in the make-up of a book is generally as follows:

Half-title and blank page.
Full title and blank page or copyright notice.
Dedication and blank page.
Preface or Introduction.[1]
Table of Contents.
List of Illustrations.
Text.
Appendix.
Glossary.
Bibliography.[2]
Index.

Errata are usually noted on the last leaf of a book or on an insert.

---

[1] The Introduction is sometimes included in the text.

[2] The Bibliography or List of Authorities Consulted is often put after the Table of Contents or the List of Illustrations.

CHAPTER IX

TECHNICAL TERMS

ANTIQUE.—Type in which the lines are heavy and of uniform thickness, the serifs, or short lines at the top and the bottom of the letter, being correspondingly heavy: **antique type**.

Black Letter.—A distorted form of the roman letter, angles taking the place of curves. In working on parchment that kinked or on paper that was rough, copyists probably found it difficult to follow all the curves of the roman character, and therefore formed the letter by repeated strokes, which caused an angular joining of the lines. The English name of black letter was not given to the character until after the introduction of roman printing-types. Old English and German Text are called by printers Black Letter.

This character is known by bibliographers as gothic, because it has always been preferred by people of Gothic descent.

Body.—The size of a type considered down a page, at right angles with the printed lines; as, pica body, long-primer body, etc.—The rectangular piece of metal on which the face of a type rests.

Bold Face.—A type with heavy lines, resembling roman. The heavy lines are made thicker, while the light lines are left untouched.

BROCHURE.—A small pamphlet, or a brief treatise in pamphlet form, on a matter of transitory interest.— An unbound book, the sheets of which are stitched together and covered with a wrapper.

CAPITALS.—The largest letters of a font. They vary in size, according to the font of type used.

CASE.—A frame with a set of boxes, containing assorted type. The compositor, as he works, has before him two inclined cases, one above the other, called, respectively, Upper Case and Lower Case.

CHASE.—The rectangular frame which incloses a form of type.

COLOPHON.—An inscription or imprint placed at the end of a book, generally giving the title, the writer's or the printer's name, and the date and the place of publication. This method of denoting the printer and the place of printing, which was common in the early period of the art, passed out of use entirely in the eighteenth century. It has been revived, to some extent, in artistic printing.

COMPOSING.—Setting type.

COMPOSING STICK.—A three-sided tray in which types are set by the compositor, or "composed."

CONDENSED.—A type having the horizontal lines shorter than in ordinary type. Extra-condensed.—A type still narrower than condensed.

COPY.—Manuscript or typewritten matter to be printed, or matter already in printed form to be reprinted.

CUT-IN LETTER.—A letter of a size larger than

the type of the page, which is adjusted at the beginning of the first paragraph of a chapter.

CUT-IN NOTE.—A note justified into the side of a paragraph. The letters of a cut-in note are always much smaller than the type of the page. An extra price must be paid for this work, as it is very troublesome and requires much time.

DISPLAYED.—Having various kinds and sizes of type well-selected, arranged, and spaced. In display matter, the important topics are put in separate lines.

DISTRIBUTE.—To return types to their respective boxes in the cases, after printing. This term is applied also to spreading ink evenly over the surface of a roller on the press.

DUMMY.—A few pages of a book, or a portion of a newspaper or a magazine, put together before the entire work is issued, as a specimen of the size and appearance of the real publication. Canvassers are supplied with dummies of the works they sell.

DUODECIMO.—A term denoting that the sheet has been folded in twelve leaves or twenty-four pages. —A book printed, originally, with twelve leaves to the sheet, but now usually having sixteen leaves to the sheet. Abbreviated 12mo or 12°. It has been the practice to print 12° with 24 pages to the sheet, and then cut off eight pages and fold them in as an inset. Some presses are now made large enough, however, to print thirty-two, sixty-four, or even a larger number of pages at a time. 24° is simply 12° doubled. In book-work, duodecimo, octavo, quarto, etc., no longer indicate fixed dimensions, as sheets of paper vary greatly in size.

EM.—The square of the body of a type. The amount of matter composed is estimated by ems.

EVEN PAGES OR FOLIOS.—Pages bearing the even numbers, 2, 4, 6, 8, etc. They are the left-hand pages of a printed work.

EXPANDED—Extended.—Type having the horizontal lines longer than the standard width. These two terms are used synonymously by type-founders.

FOLIO.—Consisting of two leaves or four pages, the sheet having been folded but once.—A book in which the sheet has been folded in two leaves or four pages.—In *Law*, a certain number of words, which is the unit for estimating the length of a document; in the United States, the unit is 100 words, in English parliamentary proceedings, 90 words.—The running numbers of the pages of a book.—Folio, to number pages consecutively.

FONT.—A complete assortment of a certain size and style of type. A full font of book or newspaper type includes: roman capitals, small capitals, and lower case letters; italic capitals and italic lower case; roman and italic ligatures; figures, points and marks (punctuation marks, marks of reference, braces, dashes, leaders, and commercial signs), fractions, spaces, quadrats, accents. In books printed in England, the word is usually spelled fount.

FORWARDING.—The various processes employed in the binding of a book. The decoration of the cover is called the "finishing."

FORM.—Type arranged in pages ready for printing, in the order in which they are locked up.

FRISKET.—A thin framework of iron hinged to the upper part of the tympan of a platen-press, to keep in place the sheet to be printed.

FUDGE.—To work without proper materials. Late news, consisting of only a few lines, is set up as fudge matter and run into the space left for it.

FURNITURE.—Strips of wood or of metal used to fill the spaces around or between pages of type or plates, so as to give the proper margin.

GALLEY.—A thin frame of brass, wood and brass, type metal, or zinc, with flanges on three sides to support the type which is placed in the frame after copy has been set up.

GALLEY PROOF.—First proof or slip-proof of work, usually printed on long sheets of paper, from the type as it stands in the galley.

GERMAN TEXT.—A style of black letter.

The present distorted forms of the Latin letters arose in the middle ages and are the work of the monks. At the time of the invention of printing they were in general use in Europe, but have been finally abandoned by nearly all nations except the Germans. As with the so-called black letter in England, they are the result of an effort to reproduce in printing the forms of the letters as they appeared in the manuscripts of the monks. There is a growing preference among authors and publishers for the simpler roman characters, which furnish much less work for the type-founder and are far less injurious to the eyesight.—VALENTINE: *New High German.*

GOTHIC.—The type now known by printers as gothic is a certain style of roman without flourishes or serifs (lines at the top and the bottom of a letter), and having all the strokes of the same thickness. It seems to be an imitation of the old Roman mural letters. GOTHIC.

The characters first used by the early printers, and known by writers and bibliographers as gothic, was a form of letter which had been employed by the copyists of Europe for several centuries before the invention of movable types. From the many styles of letters used in manuscripts, the printers selected two: the pointed character, now called by French bibliographers the *lettre de forme,* and the round character, to which has been given the name of *lettre de somme.* The "Bible of Forty-two Lines" and the "Psalter" of 1457 were printed in the pointed gothic; the "Letters of Indulgence" of 1453 and 1454 and the "Catholicon" of 1460, in the round gothic. The pointed character was the standard or formal letter; the round gothic was the style preferred for ordinary books.

IMPOSING.—Arranging pages of type on the imposing stone, so that they will be in regular order when the printed sheet is folded.

IMPOSING STONE.—A stone on which the pages of type are imposed in their proper order and locked up ready for printing.

IMPRINT.—The name and address of the printer or of the publisher of a book or job-work. The imprint is placed at the foot of the title-page of a book or pamphlet, and on the back of job-work.

INDENTION.—The setting back of a line from the margin. In a Hanging Indention the first line begins at the margin and the other lines are set back. A common indention is one *m*. The indentation, however, depends upon the width of the matter, and whether it is leaded or solid.

INSET.—One sheet placed inside of another and both folded. In newspaper work, inserted or "inset" means that the sheets are delivered folded one inside the other, as the sheets are arranged in a quire of writing-paper, but not necessarily pasted, although this is generally done. When, instead of all the sheets being placed one inside the other, the sections are laid one on top of the other, full-page size, and are then folded together to half-page size, the method is called "collecting." In bookwork an inset is an offcut or supplementary leaf not included in the regular form.

ITALIC LETTER.—A letter inclining to the right, introduced by Aldus Manutius. It is said to be an imitation of the handwriting of Petrarch. [See ITALIC LETTER, page 156.]

JOB-WORK.—All the miscellaneous matter of a printing-office beyond book and newspaper work. [See JOB-WORK, page 42.]

JUSTIFY.—To space out lines according to a given length, so that they shall be neither too long nor too short.

KERNED LETTER.—A letter in which a part of the face projects over the body, as in the italic *f*, which is kerned at both ends.

LEADS.—Thin strips of metal used for separating lines of type. Matter composed without leads is termed *solid*. A page widely leaded has a handsomer appearance and is more legible than one in which the lines are close together.

LEADERS.—Dots or hyphens which lead the eye from the end of a line to figures or references in indexes, contents, tables, accounts, etc.—Editorial articles in daily newspapers.

LETTERPRESS.—A term given to type-work to distinguish it from lithographic work and steel and copperplate printing.

LET-IN NOTE.—The same as cut-in note.

LIGATURE.—Two or more letters cast together on the same shank. This is done when one letter has a part of its face hanging over one or both sides of its shank, and, consequently, if used alone would be battered when locked up against the shank of another letter. The ligatures are ff, fi, fl, ffi, ffl, lb., and, in old style, ct. The diphthongs æ and œ are also ligatures.

LIGHT FACE.—Type in which the heavy lines are but little thicker than the fine strokes.

LOCKING UP.—Tightening up a form of work after it is paged, so that it may be lifted from the imposing stone without the type or the furniture dropping out.

LOGOTYPE.—Two or more letters cast on one shank. The same as Ligature.

LOWER CASE.—The lower tray or case next the compositor. It contains the small letters and other characters. By lower-case letters is meant small letters; by upper-case letters, capitals.

MAKING READY.—This term includes all the processes of "underlaying" and "overlaying" which the pressman must employ, to bring the forms of type and cuts practically parallel with the impression-cylinder, so as to produce a perfectly satisfactory impression on the sheet of paper.

MAKING UP.—Preparing type in regular order for printing. This includes: adjusting the interior spacing, putting in the proper head-bands and foot-lines, imposing the pages on the stone, placing around them the chase and the furniture, and, finally, locking up the pages.

MODERN FACE.—A style of roman type which has been cast since the beginning of the nineteenth century, and which is more regular and even and has less angular serifs than preceding styles.

NICK.—A cut made in the front of a type to indicate to the compositor how it should be placed in the stick. Nicks also distinguish one font from another.

OCTAVO.—Having eight leaves or sixteen pages to a sheet. Abbreviated 8vo. or 8°.

ODD PAGES OR FOLIOS.—Pages bearing the odd numbers, 1, 3, 5, 7, etc. They are the right-hand pages.

OLD ENGLISH.—A name given by book-lovers to a certain style of black letter, which resembles the characters first used after the invention of printing.

OLD STYLE.—A style of roman type in general use in the eighteenth century; called also "old face." It fell into disuse in England and America at the beginning of the nineteenth century, but was revived about 1843. MODERNIZED OLD STYLE, or MEDIEVAL, is a type more regular in form than the original old style.

OVERLAY.—A sheet or piece of paper placed between the sheet to be printed and the impression surface, to bring out the proper effects.

OVERRUN.—To carry matter backwards or forwards from one line to another, or from one page to another. This is necessary when something is to be omitted or new matter is to be inserted. Overrunning is a very slow operation, as a whole paragraph, or even several pages, must sometimes be readjusted before the necessary space can be gained or lost.

PAGINATION.—The numerical sequence of the pages.

PI.—Type broken down or indiscriminately mixed.

PLATEN.—The flat part or "plate" of a press, which is brought down upon the form of type to make the impression.

POINTS.—The comma, semicolon, colon, period, mark of interrogation, mark of exclamation, hyphen, apostrophe, parenthesis, and bracket. "Point" is employed also to indicate a certain size of type.

PROOF.—An impression of composed matter, taken to ascertain its correctness.

Office Proof is the first proof taken from composed types. It is read by the proof-reader of the printing-office, and is corrected by the compositor at his own expense.

Author's Proof is the clean proof drawn after the corrections indicated in the office proof have been made; this clean proof is sent with the manuscript to the author.

Galley Proof is proof taken from the type in the galley, and in any extended work it is usually printed on long sheets of paper called galleys. This is generally the first "author's proof."

Revised or *Second Proof* is one drawn after the corrections indicated in the first "author's proof" have been made by the compositor.

Paged Proof is a proof of paged matter arranged on the imposing stone, according to the paging desired.

Foundry Proof is one taken after the corrections indicated in the last "author's proof" have been made, and before the forms are sent to the foundry to be cast.

Plate Proof is a proof drawn after the plates have been cast, and which, if the author so desires, he may see for inspection, and verification of the final changes made.

Foul Proof is one which contains more errors than would be made by a skilful and careful compositor.

ᴌOOF PAPER.—A cheap paper on which the impressions of printed work are made. The author must not suppose that it is a sample of the paper on which the work will appear when completed. The special kind and quality of paper desired for the publication in its final form should be definitely stated by the person giving the order.

QUADRAT or QUAD.—A short blank piece of metal, lower than the type, used for spacing at the beginning of a paragraph or between sentences, and to fill up blank places. The em quadrat, or the square of the body of the type, is the basis of computation for all spaces and quadrats, and for the measurement of composition; it is also the unit for measuring the fatness or leanness of type. An en quad is half the size of an em quad. There are also two-em and three-em quads. "Quad" is the only term used in printing offices; its plural is quads.

QUARTO.—Having four leaves or eight pages to a sheet.

RECTO.—The right side of a leaf, which has the odd folio.

REGISTER.—The adjustment of pages, so that they shall be printed back to back, the edges coinciding.—The printing in their proper places of colors distributed on plates attached to the cylinder of a press.

ROMAN.—An upright type used in printing in England and America and in all the countries whose languages are derived from the Latin. In manuscript the roman letter was employed until about the close of the twelfth century. Roman type was first cast in 1465 by two German printers, Sweinheym and Pannartz, at Subiaco, Italy. It was afterwards perfected and used by Nicolas Jenson, at Venice, in 1471.

Although in *printed* works, the gothic character preceded the roman, the latter had been employed in *manuscripts* many centuries before the introduction of the gothic letter. Gothic letter, in fact, was formed on the roman.

SCRIPT.—Inclined letters which resemble the modern or the Italian handwriting.

SEPARATRIX.—A diagonal stroke used in proofreading, to separate the corrections in the margin, when several errors occur in one line.

SEPARATUM.—A separate copy or reprint of a paper forming one in a series, as in the printed report of the proceedings of a scientific body. Papers of specialists are generally issued as *separata*, for the benefit of persons who are interested only in the subjects therein treated, and who do not care for the full report of the proceedings.

SERIFS.—The short cross-lines at the top and bottom of a letter: M.

SHANK.—The rectangular metal body upon which the face of a type rests.

SIGNATURE.—A figure or letter placed at the foot of each sheet of a volume, to indicate to the binder the order in which the sheets are to follow each other in the completed book. Each sheet has its own figure or letter.—The sheet bearing such a figure or letter, considered as a fractional part of the whole work; thus, we say that a volume is printed in sixteen signatures. [See SIGNATURES, page 64.

Skeleton.—Type in which the lines are very thin and have little weight. Skeleton type may be of almost any style, and may be either condensed or extended

Slug.—A thick piece of type-metal used for spacing out, also as a foot-line.

Small Capitals.—Letters having the same form as capitals, but smaller in size. They are used for headings of chapters, running headlines, for headings in divisions of a subject, and to give greater emphasis to a word or words than italic letters would convey.

Solid.—Type set up without leads.

Sorts.—The letters belonging to one box of a case, as distinguished from a complete font.

Spaces.—Short blank pieces of metal used to separate one word from another, and for small blanks in lines, in order to make them of uniform length. Spaces are lower than the type and should make no impression on the paper.

Stock.—A special kind and quality of paper.

Superior Characters.—Small letters, figures, or characters cast upon the upper part of the shank of a type, and, consequently, when printed, slightly above the range of letters in the line; in ordinary printing, they serve as reference marks. In correcting proof, a superior character, when placed in the margin, should be enclosed (a right or an acute angle is generally used) to prevent its being placed on a range with the letters of the line.

Take.—The amount of copy which is given out at one time to be composed.

Tympan.—A framed appliance hinged to the

upper end of the bed of a platen-press. It receives the sheet to be printed, and softens and equalizes the pressure by means of blankets between its two parts.

UPPER CASE.—The upper of the two cases before the compositor. It contains capitals, small capitals, and other marks.

VERSICLE.—One of a series of short verses said or sung alternately by the minister or officiant and the choir or people. The name is sometimes given specifically to one of the lines said just after the creed. In prayer-books the liturgical sign of the versicle is ℣.

VERSO.—The left side of a leaf, or the page which has the even folio.

WHITE PAGE.—A blank page.

REPRODUCTIVE PROCESSES

CHAPTER I

STEREOTYPING AND ELECTROTYPING

STEREOTYPES are plates of type-metal and are made by casting; electrotypes are produced by galvanic action.

Stereotyping and electrotyping have proved a source of great economy to both the author and the publisher. Before the discovery of these processes, a work to be printed as occasion required had to be kept standing in type or else reset for each edition. By electrotyping the forms, only a small number of the first edition need be printed, as additional copies can be taken off at any time. The plates occupy much less space than type matter kept in form, and can easily be stored away for future use. The printer's type is released for other work, which in itself is a decided advantage. These two processes also save wear of the original type or cut. Electrotypes have superseded stereotypes for book and magazine work, as they give a clearer impression and are more durable.

Three methods of stereotyping are known: the plaster, the clay, and the papier-maché. Only the last is now much employed.

The process of casting type-metal in moulds of plaster-of-paris was discovered by William Ged, a goldsmith of Edinburgh, who began his experiments about 1725. His method proved successful, but he could not get the printers to use his plates. Numerous experiments followed, but all other methods were finally superseded by that of the Earl of Stanhope, which was introduced about 1804. The plaster process served for types on book-work for about fifty years, but it was unsuitable for engravings, and was found too slow for daily newspapers.

The first work stereotyped in America was the Westminster Catechism, the plates for which were produced in New York, by John Watts, in 1813. Watts, however, sold out and went to Austria in 1816. The introduction of the art into America was really due to David Bruce, one of the two brothers who afterwards established the type-foundry known by that name. In 1813 Bruce returned from England, where he had been endeavoring to study the methods of Lord Stanhope; he began his experiments, and in 1814 succeeded in casting plates for the New Testament.

The papier-maché process. The papier-maché process was discovered by Genoux of France, in 1829, and was introduced into Great Britain in 1832.

In the papier-maché process, a paper matrix is first made of the page of type by machinery. The material for the matrix is formed by pasting together layers of thick unsized paper and tissue paper, each layer being carefully rolled smooth with a heavy iron roller. The matrix is dried by steam-heat; to expel any remaining moisture, it is exposed for half a minute either in an oven or to the flame of a gas-jet. After the edges are trimmed, the matrix is placed in the casting-box and filled with melted metal. On being removed from the casting-box, the superfluous metal is cut off from the plate, which is then trimmed by hand and shaved on the reverse side, to bring it to the exact thickness required. These operations are performed by machinery.

The papier-maché process is far more expeditious than any other method. A matrix and four stereotype plates can be made in seven minutes; it is possible to cast a plate a minute after the matrix is made. Curved plates can be made as easily as flat, and as many as forty plates can be cast from the same matrix. This process has been adopted by all large daily newspapers.

Electrotypes are plates produced by means of electricity; they are made from type, woodcuts, and engraved plates. The process of causing one metal to be deposited on another by galvanic action is not new, but the electrotyping of type, woodcuts, and plates is of comparatively recent date. An engraving made by this method appeared in the *London Journal* for April, 1840. In America Joseph A. Adams, a wood-engraver of New York, produced plates which were used in *Mapes's Magazine* as early as 1841. Before 1855 the art of electrotyping was in general use in New York {.sidenote} Electrotypes.

To make an electrotype plate, copper, placed in a state of solution, is caused by electric action to {.sidenote} The process of electrotyping.

spread itself over the surface of a mould and there be deposited in a sheet.

A wax mould is first made of the engraved plate or type. To produce this, beeswax is poured on a leaden slab and is left to cool, after which graphite is brushed evenly over the surface.

The form of type or the plate is forced into the wax by means of a steam-press. This gives a mould of the type or plate in the wax. The surplus wax is removed with a sharp knife.

As the mould comes out uneven, it has to be built up; this is done by filling the large blank spaces and the surfaces between the lines with hot wax, so that the deposits of copper may be shallow. The mould is then given a coat of graphite in the black-leading machine. The graphite makes the mould a conductor of electricity.

After the deposit of this metallic surface, the superfluous graphite is washed out with water. Iron filings are sifted on the mould and a weak solution of sulphate of copper is stirred in. This coating of copper is given to facilitate the plating. To make the electrical connection, a piece of copper or lead is imbedded in the edge of the sheet of wax.

The mould is then suspended for one or two hours in a bath of sulphate of copper solution. By the action of the electric current, the coating is increased until it is about .005 of an inch thick.

The shell of copper is removed from the wax and is washed in boiling water. It is brushed on the back with a solution of chloride of zinc, and sheets of tinfoil are laid over it and melted. Enough molten lead is poured on it to give the plate the necessary thickness—about one-eighth of an inch. An airblast causes the plate to cool and solidify immediately.

Any defects or indentations on the face of the plate are hammered up from the back, and it is afterward passed through machines which finish it and give it a bevel on the side. After the plate is mounted, it is ready for the press. A plate to be used on a web perfecting-press is given a curvature to fit it to the cylinder. When red ink is used, electrotypes are usually given a coating of nickel, to protect the copper from the action of the mercury.

An electrotype plate will stand from five hundred thousand to six hundred thousand impressions. A stereotype plate lasts for only about one hundred thousand impressions. Both stereotype and electrotype plates are now sometimes made as large as two pages of a newspaper.

By hurrying each step of the process, it is possible to make an electrotype plate in an hour; but for a high grade of work more care is taken, and it then requires several hours to produce a plate with fine finish.

The price of electrotyping is from one to three cents a square inch. Line work costs about seven cents, and half-tones from twelve to fifteen cents a square inch.

CHAPTER II

HALF-TONE AND LINE ENGRAVING

THE numerous illustrations which give life and add to the value of our books, magazines, and newspapers,[1] without greatly increasing their cost, have been brought into existence by the development of the relatively new art of photo-engraving, which by 1880 was beginning to supplant the reproducing of wood-cuts. Reproductions of photographs, wash-drawings, paintings, or of any picture or object in which there is a gradation of color, are made by the half-tone process. Drawings or pictures consisting of simple lines, that is without tones of color, such as pen sketches or fac-similes of old writings, are reproduced by line-plates.

An illustration printed from a line-plate resembles a pen and ink drawing; that is, it consists simply of lines. A half-tone has no lines at all: it is composed of dots, and has middle tones, full tones, and high lights.

---

[1] The illustration of English journals dates back to 1832, when the *Penny Magazine*, a periodical somewhat of the nature of a popularized cyclopedia, was first published; but illustrated journalism did not fairly begin until *The Illustrated London News* was founded in 1842. *Gleason's Pictorial* was started in Boston about 1850. *Frank Leslie's* followed in 1854, and *Harper's Weekly* in 1857. The first illustrated daily paper in America was *The Daily Graphic* of New York, established in 1873.

HALF-TONE REPRODUCTION—STATUE OF GUTENBERG AT STRASBURG.
[From a Photograph.]

HALF-TONE AND LINE ENGRAVING

To produce a half-tone, a negative is made of the picture by the wet collodion process, with the use of a screen, and a copperplate is made of this negative. Line-plates are prepared by the same process without the use of a screen, and are made of zinc. In newspaper work, both half-tone and line plates are produced by zinc etching, as copper requires too much time.

If a plain negative of a photograph were printed and etched on metal and then mounted the proper height and placed on a printing-press, the impression taken from it would be entirely black and white, the shades being black and the high lights white. There would be no relief to the black portions, and the white parts would be etched entirely away. A printing-plate must have these parts broken up in some way, so that the light and the dark parts may be given their proper values. In the half-tone process, this is accomplished by the use of a transparent screen, generally of glass, which consists of two plates and on which have been made fine lines, the lines of one plate intersecting those of the other at right angles. This screen is placed in the plate-holder, in front of the negative, and the rays of light passing through it break up the parts in such a way as to show the gradation of color. When the lines are close together the engraving will be finer than when a coarse screen is used, but it will be more difficult to print. One hundred and thirty or forty lines to the inch is the average number. *Half-tones.*

To produce a line-plate, a negative is first made

from the photograph or sketch, and is developed
plates. in the dark-room. A plate of zinc is sensitized
with a solution consisting of bichromate of ammonium (or potassium), distilled water, and albumen. This solution is poured several times over
the plate. The sensitizing is done in the dark-room,
and the zinc plate is then placed in the printing-frame.
The plate is laid flat upon the negative and the crossbars are screwed down very tight, to insure perfect
contact. Exposure to strong light, either sunlight
or electric light, from two to eight minutes, then
follows; the light passes through the transparent
parts and prints on the metal. Nothing shows on
the plate when it is taken out of the printing-frame.
It is rolled with printer's or lithographic transfer-ink,
and is laid face upwards in a tray containing enough
water barely to cover its surface. The plate is afterwards rubbed very gently with a piece of clean
absorbent cotton, which removes the superfluous ink.
The print appears in the form of black lines against
a bright background. The ink clings to the parts
acted on by the light; it rubs away the parts not
acted on and leaves the plain metal. After the plate
has been washed and heated, it is powdered with
dragon's blood, which protects the lines of the engraving when the plate is etched in the acid bath.
In the etching all the parts not so protected are eaten
away, the lines being left in relief. The etching
solution is composed of nitric acid and water. In
ordinary commercial work, three or four baths, sometimes more, are necessary before the plate acquires

REPRODUCTION FROM LINE-PLATE—OLD WOODEN PRINTING-PRESS, 1508.

[After Wood-Cut by Badius.]

the proper depth; for newspaper work the plate is given from two to four bites, as time permits.

Routing. The next step is the routing, or drilling. On the routing-machine, in the parts where the acid did not bite deep enough, the plate is still further cut away, and large parts which are not to show at all are removed. The plate is then mounted, or nailed to a block, and is ready for the composing-room. In printing from the plate on the press, the projecting parts show black and the indentations white.

The films. The body-work, or background, of an illustration is sometimes produced by rubbing the plate, before it is etched, through films which are made of a preparation of gelatine and which are inked. By placing films on parts of the plate to be strengthened, and gently rubbing on the back of the film, various lines or dots are produced. The films are so made as to give different shades of color to a plate—small dots and fine lines for delicate tones, heavy lines and large dots for deeper tones. The stipple-work which forms the background of colored illustrations in news- is produced in this way.

Printing half-tones on copper. In printing a half-tone on copper, the plate is sensitized in a silver bath instead of a solution of bichromate of ammonium. The etching mordant is perchloride of iron instead of nitric acid.

In reproducing a sketch or illustration, better effects can be obtained by using a sketch or cut which is large in size and reducing it to the dimensions desired. In reducing the dimensions, the intensity of the blackness of the lines is increased; in enlarging an illustration. the lines would appear fainter.

Making plates for newspaper work.

As stated above, for newspaper illustration, both half-tone and line work are printed on zinc. Both plates are produced in about the same way as for books and magazines, except that in newspaper work each step of the process is performed with greater rapidity. Daily journals have many little devices for facilitating the work: they spend less time in making the negative and use an electric fan for drying. For book or magazine work, several hours are required to make a plate carefully; a newspaper produces a plate in an hour. If a fire or some unusual occurrence takes place a little before midnight, a sketch artist is sent out, a cut is made, and the illustration appears in the two o'clock edition of the paper.

Plates for colored pictures

The plates for colored pictures, with which many of our newspaper supplements are illustrated, are prepared by about the same process as an ordinary line-plate; the main difference consists in making a separate plate for each color, as on the press the paper passes from one cylinder to another to receive the various colors.

"Making-ready."

In order to obtain a perfectly satisfactory impression on the sheet to be printed, so that all the letters shall be clearly and distinctly printed, one part of the sheet being no blacker or fainter in color than any other part, the pressman is obliged to resort to a series of experiments or processes which are known by the general term of "making ready." The first impression is never perfect, as the faces of types and plates are never exactly on the same

HALF-TONE AND LINE ENGRAVING 91

level, and, unless the press is new, the surface of the impression-cylinder is probably worn by constant use. The types and the plates must be made practically parallel with the impression-cylinder, so that the force of the pressure on the sheet shall be in every part, as nearly as possible, the same.

This evening up process is accomplished by using "underlays" and "overlays" of paper. The preparation of the overlays for fine illustrated work is a complicated and difficult operation, and requires much care and experience on the part of the pressman. Pieces of thin paper, but little thicker than tissue paper, are pasted on the impression-cylinder, in places where the pressure is too light. Hundreds of these pieces of paper are often used before the irregularities can be overcome and a satisfactory impression produced. It sometimes requires two or three days' labor on the part of the pressman, to bring out the blacks, the half-tints, and the high lights as they should appear in the picture.

"Underlays" and "overlays."

For newspaper work, a line-plate is locked up with the form of type, which is set by the linotype and which is the size of one full page of the paper, and is stereotyped with the type. To get a clear impression of the cut, in making the matrix, an overlay, or piece of stiff prepared paper, is placed directly over the plate, so as to keep it down as tight as possible.

Printing from plates in newspaper work.

Matrices are made from half-tones, but in order to get better effects, some newspapers print directly from the plate itself, as is done in fine work. A depression or space is left in the matrix and the half-tone is inserted into it; when the molten lead is poured over the matrix, the cut is soldered into the stereotype plate. To save wear, half-tones are nickel-plated for color work, as nickel is not easily affected by colored inks. A plate to be used on a web-press is made with a curve which fits it to the cylinder. In printing a half-tone, a paper or overlay is placed between the sheet and the impression-cylinder, so as to bring out the lights and shades that should appear in the picture.

PUNCTUATION

CHAPTER I

IN punctuating, one aim should be kept in view—to use such marks and only such as are needed to make clear the writer's meaning. It should be borne in mind that a mark of punctuation is not always needed where a pause would be required in reading or speaking. The office of punctuation is to indicate the grammatical construction and the sense. While it is necessary to have some general rules governing the subject, no intelligent person will confine himself strictly to them. One who understands the exact meaning of a passage, even if he has but a general knowledge of the use of the marks, will punctuate far better than he who blindly follows a "rule." Points which, according to certain rules, would be employed in some cases, in others are better omitted, as commas in long complex sentences containing many clauses. On the other hand, it is often necessary to insert a comma or other mark not required by rule, to prevent ambiguity.

The principal punctuation marks are: the period (.), colon (:), semicolon (;), comma (,), interrogation point (?), exclamation point (!), dash (—), marks of parenthesis ( ), brackets [ ], quotation marks (" "), apostrophe ('), and hyphen (-).

THE PERIOD

1. Ends of Sentences.

The period should be used at the end of every sentence which is complete in itself and which is declarative, imperative, or but slightly exclamatory.

I will work in my own sphere, nor wish it other than it is. This alone is health and happiness. This alone is life.—LONGFELLOW: *Hyperion.*

Love thy neighbor as thyself.

A wide freedom, truly.

2. Abbreviated Words.

A period is generally placed after an abbreviation; as, M. D., Esq., viz. for *videlicet* (namely), e. g. for *exempli gratia* (for example), etc. A period should not be used after a word in which the omission of letters is indicated by an apostrophe; as, dec'd for deceased.

When a sentence ends with an abbreviated word, only one point is needed.

So far as possible, the use of two points together should be avoided. The period may be omitted after a colon or an interrogation point following an abbreviation.

The lecture will be given on Thursday, at 4 p. m. Has he the degree of Ph.D?

Names which are merely a shortening of a proper name should not be followed by a period; as, Ben, Will, Bess.

A period should not be placed after such abbreviations of dates as 1st, 2d, 3d, 4th, etc., unless they occur at the end of a sentence.

3. Roman Numerals and Arabic Numerals.

Roman numerals do not require to be followed by the period: Book II; chap. IV; Edward VII, Louis IX of France.

A period should be placed after roman and arabic numerals when they are used to number a table of contents, a list of subjects, paragraphs, or parts of the same paragraph.

Numbers, generally, should be written out. Arabic numerals are employed for dates, street addresses, citation of pages, in technical matter, and when figures cannot be indicated by a round number. When many numbers appear in a work, to enable the eye to catch them readily, they should be expressed by arabic numerals. Figures are generally used in commercial printing, but words are preferred for book-work and formal writing.

4. Sideheads, and Names of Works or of Authors following an Extract.

When a sidehead is placed at the beginning of a paragraph, it is followed by a period and a dash. These marks are usually placed after an extract, when the name of the author or work from which the extract is taken follows in the same paragraph. In these cases the dash is an ornamental mark used by the printer.

Mathematics.—Arithmetic, geometry, algebra.
The foundation of true joy is in the conscience.—SENECA.

5. Items of a Catalogue or Syllabus.

A period should be placed after each item of a catalogue or syllabus when the items are not closely related.

Harding, Edwards. Costume of the Russian Empire. 1811.[1]

Lecture I.—The Development of Language, Oral and Written. Ancient Systems of Writing. Derivation of the English Alphabet.

In lists of names given in columns, final periods are not used.

In a table of contents, the different topics of a paragraph are usually separated by dashes.

6. Title-pages, Headings, Cards, etc.

On title-pages, cards, and in headings of circulars, etc., the best usage is to omit the punctuation marks at the ends of the lines, except periods denoting abbreviations. The lines are sufficiently set off by the blank spaces which follow. Commas and other marks needed within the lines are employed.

NEW ORLEANS

THE PLACE AND THE PEOPLE

by

GRACE KING

Author of "Jean Baptiste le Moyne, Sieur de Bienville," "Balcony Stories," etc.

With illustrations by Frances E. Jones

New York
Macmillan and Co.
and London
1895
All rights reserved

---

[1] When such items occur in foot-notes, citations, etc., very little punctuation is employed: Cf Harleian MS Brit Mus. 3469

CHAPTER II

THE COLON

1. A Quotation, Speech, or an Enumeration of Particulars Formally introduced.

A quotation, a speech, a course of reasoning, or an enumeration of particulars when formally introduced should be preceded by a colon.

> All our conduct toward men should be influenced by this important precept: "All things whatsoever ye would that men should do to you, do ye even so to them."
>
> Lord Chatham, in his speech on the Right of Taxation, says: The gentleman [Mr. Grenville] tells us America is obstinate; America is almost in open rebellion. I rejoice that America has resisted. Three millions of people so dead to all the feelings of liberty as voluntarily to submit to be slaves, would have been fit instruments to make slaves of the rest.

When the quotation or enumeration begins a new paragraph, some writers place a dash after the colon. As the dash in this case is of no service in indicating the grammatical construction, the colon is the only mark needed.

If the quotation or enumeration is not directly introduced by the preceding sentence, a period should be used.

> We will now consider each point separately.
> (1) The nature of the measure. (2) The benefit it will confer upon the community, should it become a law. (3) Whose interests it may injure.

If the quotation is short and closely connected with what precedes, a comma before it is sufficient.

There is much in the proberb, Without pains no gains.

When an example or illustration is introduced by such a word or phrase as *as, that is, viz., namely, to wit,* etc., a semicolon is placed before and a comma after the connective word.

To Greece we are indebted for the three principal orders of architecture; namely, the Doric, the Ionic, and the Corinthian.

When the statement following is long or formal, a comma is used before the introductory word and a colon after it.

The colon is frequently used in dignified address. It is thus employed after the salutation of a letter.

Mr. President: The Honorable Gentleman from Illinois has just stated, etc.

Dear Sir:
 Your letter of the 3d instant has just reached me.

2. Statements in Apposition, and a Generic Term Followed by Specifications.

A colon should be placed between two clauses not connected by a conjunction, when the second is in some way in apposition with the first, or is added as an explanation or illustration.

The colon is used also after a general term followed by several statements in apposition with it; the statements are separated from one another by semicolons.

The darkness of death is like the evening twilight: it makes all objects appear more lovely to the dying.—RICHTER.

We hold these truths to be self-evident: that all men are created equal; that they are endowed by their Creator with certain inalienable rights; that among these are life, liberty, and the pursuit of happiness.

3. Members of a Sentence Which are Subdivided by Semicolons.

The colon is sometimes used to separate two members of a compound sentence which are subdivided by semicolons. Such cases, however, are of rare occurrence.

One's age should be tranquil, as one's childhood should be playful; hard work at either extremity of human existence seems to be out of place: the morning and the evening should be alike cool and peaceful; at midday the sun may burn, and men may labor under it.—DR. T. ARNOLD.

CHAPTER III

THE SEMICOLON

1. Members of a Compound Sentence.

The semicolon is used to separate short members of a compound sentence, when the conjunction is omitted or when the connection is not close.

There are no songs comparable to the songs of Zion; no orations equal to those of the Prophets; and no politics like those which the Scriptures teach.—MILTON.

The semicolon is used to separate members of a compound sentence which are subdivided by commas, even when the members are joined by connectives.

Books are the food of youth, the delight of old age; the ornament of prosperity, the refuge and comfort of adversity; a delight at home, and no hindrance abroad; companions by night, in traveling, in the country.—CICERO.

A Scotch mist becomes a shower; and a shower, a flood; and a flood, a storm; and a storm, a tempest, thunder, and lightning; and thunder and lightning, heavenquake and earthquake.

2. Short Sentences Related in Meaning.

The semicolon should be placed between short complete sentences related in meaning or construction, but with no grammatical dependence upon each other. In such cases it is often possible to use a period, but the discrimination of relations would not be so clearly indicated

I see the pyramids building; I hear the shoutings of the army of Alexander; I feel the ground shake beneath the march of Cambyses.—ALEXANDER SMITH.

If the sentences are short and very closely connected, commas may be used.

The drums beat, the banners unfurl, the army marches.

3. Explanatory Clauses.

A semicolon should be placed after a complete sentence followed by a clause denoting contrast, inference, or explanation, when the clause is introduced by a conjunction.

It is in vain to gather virtues without humility; for the Spirit of God delighteth to dwell in the hearts of the humble.—ERASMUS.

4. Clauses Having a Common Dependence upon another Clause.

The semicolon is used to separate clauses which have a common dependence upon another clause, either at the beginning or the end of the sentence.

If the clause upon which the series depends precedes, it should be separated from the first clause of the series by a comma; if it comes at the end of the sentence, a dash is placed after the last clause of the series.

The great tendency and purpose of poetry is, to carry the mind above and beyond the beaten, dusty, weary walks of ordinary life; to lift it into a purer element; and to breathe into it more profound and generous emotion.

The great golden elms that marked the line of the village street, and under whose shadows no beggars sat; the air of comfort and plenty, of neatness, thrift, and equality visible everywhere, and from far-off farms the sound of flails, beating the triumphal march of Ceres through the land—these were the sights and sounds that greeted him as he looked.— LONGFELLOW: *Kavanagh.*

It has been the custom to place a comma before the dash, when the clause upon which the series depends comes at the end of the sentence, but two punctuation marks are not needed.

5. Words Used to Introduce Examples.

As, viz., e. g., i. e., etc., or the full words for which these abbreviations stand, when used to introduce examples or illustrations, are generally preceded by the semicolon and followed by the comma, unless the connection is very close.

Greece has given us three great historians; namely, Herodotus, Xenophon, and Thucydides.

When such examples are introduced parenthetically, commas should be used.

The word 'reck,' that is, *care,* denotes a stretching of the mind.

Many of our great men, for instance, Franklin, Lincoln, and Grant, have been poor in youth.

CHAPTER IV

THE COMMA

1. Words in a Series.

When more than two words of the same part of speech or more than two phrases, in the same grammatical construction, form a series, a comma should be placed after each word or phrase except the last.

> He looked upon the world as a glad, bright, glorious world.
> No sleep so beautiful and calm, so free from trace of pain, so fair to look upon.—DICKENS.

When the last two words or phrases are connected by a conjunction, a comma should be placed before the conjunction. The use of the conjunction does not make the connection between the last two words or phrases any closer than the connection between the other words or phrases of the series. The conjunction, therefore, does not take the place of a comma.

> Alfred the Great was a brave, pious, and patriotic prince.

If the conjunction is omitted between the last two words or phrases, a comma should be placed after each word or phrase in the series, unless the last word or phrase is followed by a single word or is very closely connected with the remainder of the sentence.

> The colleges, the clergy, the lawyers, were against me.
> Teach, urge, threaten, lecture him.

Two words or phrases standing in the same relation and connected by a conjunction do not require a comma.

Reason and virtue answer one great aim.

When the conjunction is decidedly disjunctive, or when words or phrases are contrasted antithetically or are made emphatic, the comma is used before the conjunction.

He could write, and cipher too.
The vain are easily obliged, and easily disobliged.
He, and he only, is worthy of our supreme affections.

In a series of words of the same part of speech, or in a series of short phrases, connected by conjunctions, no comma is necessary.

Let us freely drink in the soul of love and beauty and wisdom from all nature and art and history.
All that charms the eye or the ear or the imagination or the heart is the gift of God.

If one of the series of words connected by conjunctions is qualified by a word or phrase which does not qualify the others, a comma should be placed before the conjunction which precedes the word thus qualified.

The men wore breeches and long boots, and frock-coats with large metal buttons; the women, straw hats, and gay calico gowns with short waists and scant folds.

2. **Conjoined Words.**

If the conjunction is omitted between two words of the same part of speech and in the same grammatical construction, they should be separated by a comma.

>Rash, fruitless war is only splendid murder.
>We are fearfully, wonderfully made.

Commas are required only between words which are coordinate in value. When adjectives which precede the object qualify other words as well as the object, commas should not be used.

>He is a bright, trustworthy young man.
>She wore a faded old shawl.
>He had beautiful large blue eyes.

In the last example, *blue* qualifies *eyes*, *large* qualifies the phrase *blue eyes*, and *beautiful* qualifies the phrase *large blue eyes*.

The comma is used to separate words repeated for the sake of emphasis.

>Verily, verily, I say unto you.
>Alone, alone, all, all alone,
>Alone on a wide, wide sea.

3. Words in Pairs.

Words or phrases used in pairs, connected by conjunctions or other particles, require a comma after each pair.

>The wise and the foolish, the weak and the strong, the young and the old, have one common Father.

>The sunny morning and the gloomy midnight, the bleak winter and the balmy spring, alike speak to us of the Creator's power.

4. Words or Phrases in Contrast.

The comma should be used to separate words or phrases in the same clause contrasted with each other.

> Speak for, not against, the principles of love and peace.
> Truth is not a stagnant pool, but a fountain.
> Rhetoric is the science, and oratory the art, of speaking well.

5. Correlative Clauses.

Two correlative clauses are separated by a comma. When the clauses are joined by *as* or *than*, the comma is omitted.

> The more diligent you are, the sooner you will accomplish your task.
> The deeper the well, the cooler the water.
> No one is so much alone in the universe as a denier of God.

6. Words or Phrases in Apposition.

Words or phrases in apposition should be separated from each other and from the rest of the sentence by commas.

> Newton, the great mathematician, was very modest.

If one of the words used is merely a general title, the comma should not be employed.

> The Emperor Augustus was a patron of the fine arts.
> The great orator Cicero was famed for many excellences.
> The river Thames

When a pronoun is used with a noun for the sake of emphasis or in direct address, the comma should be omitted.

> I myself.   Ye men of Athens.

When two or more words can be regarded as one name or as a single phrase, a comma should not be used between them.

Philip of Macedon.   Lord Chief Justice.   Our Lord Jesus Christ.   The Lord God Almighty.

Louis IX of France.   David Bruce of New York.

A title or a degree should be separated by a comma from the noun which it follows.

John James, Secretary.

Frederick W. Farrar, D.D., F.R.S.

7. Transposed Phrases or Clauses.

A phrase or clause at the beginning of a sentence which could be placed either at the end or in some other part of the sentence without changing the meaning, should be followed by a comma.

To be frank with you, the matter does not please me.

Like flakes of snow that fall unperceived upon the earth, the seemingly unimportant events of life succeed one another. —BENTHAM.

The firmest friendships have been formed in mutual adversity, as iron is most strongly united by the fiercest flame.

When the introductory phrase or clause is very short, the comma is not used, unless needed to prevent confusion.

In the year 800 Charlemagne was crowned Emperor of Rome.

In America printing began in the city of Mexico.

To the good, death presents no terrors.

8. Parenthetical Words, Phrases, and Clauses.

A word, phrase, or clause introduced loosely in a sentence and which could be omitted without destroying the meaning, is generally preceded and followed by the comma.

He promised, however, to set about a reform at once.

Dismiss, as soon as may be, all angry and wrathful thoughts.

It is mind, after all, which does the work of the world.

Human experience, like the sternlights of a ship at sea, illumines only the path which we have passed over.—COLERIDGE.

Then, now, too, also, however, therefore, consequently, accordingly, etc., are often used parenthetically. Many writers omit the commas before and after such parenthetical words as *then, too, also, indeed,* etc.: this also is desirable; that was indeed a wise measure. When any one of these words is used to modify a single word, it should not be separated from the word which it modifies.

Then I trusted him; *now* I do not.
The people are *too* credulous.

When a clause is introduced between two important parts of a sentence and is essential to its full meaning, or when a clause is thrown out of its normal place, it should be separated from the rest of the sentence by commas.

The little that is known, and the circumstance that little is known, must be considered as honorable to him.

Let us, for argument's sake, assume this.

9. Participial and Adjective Phrases.

Participial and adjective phrases are set off by commas.

The boy, laughing merrily, ran down the street.
The choral anthem, solemn and impressive, was heard through the open door.

10. Relative Clauses.

Relative clauses are introduced by relative pronouns and are either restrictive or non-restrictive. Non-restrictive clauses are preceded by the comma, and if they occur in the middle of a sentence, they are followed by this mark. Restrictive clauses do not take commas. The antecedent of a restrictive clause is generally modified by *a, the,* or *that.*

Cherish true patriotism, which has its root in benevolence.
The eye, that sees all things, sees not itself.
His stories, which made everybody laugh, were often made to order.
The lever which moves the world of mind is emphatically the printing-press.
A man who has never been at sea cannot be thoroughly proficient in navigation.

A comma should be placed before the pronoun of a restrictive clause, when the relative refers to each noun in a series.

He had hopes, fears, and longings, which his friends could not share.

11. Subject and Predicate.

If the subject of a sentence is so long that the reader might find difficulty in separating it from the predicate, or if the nominative ends with a word which might be read with the predicate and thus confound the sense, a comma may be placed after the subject.

That a peculiar state of the mere particles of the brain should be followed by a change of the state of the sentient mind, is truly wonderful.

To walk beneath the porch, is still infinitely less than to kneel before the cross.

If the subject ends with a verb and the predicate also begins with one, a comma should be placed between them.

Whatever is, is right.

12. Long Infinitive Phrases.

A long infinitive phrase, whether used as subject or occurring at the end of a sentence, is set off by a comma.

To pull down the false and build up the true, let this be our endeavor.

And Freedom shall awhile repair,
To dwell, a weeping hermit, there.

13. Adverbs and Adverbial Phrases.

When adverbs or adverbial phrases modify clauses or sentences, they should be separated from the rest of the sentence by a comma.

Next, we know that parties must ever exist in a free country.—EDMUND BURKE.

Let us, in the first place, observe the inanimate world.

In short sentences the comma is omitted.

Be ready when I come.

14. Such Clauses as It is Said, We are Told, etc.,
when used to introduce several statements, each preceded by the word *that*, should be separated from the rest of the sentence by a comma. If there is but one proposition, the comma should not be used.

Philosophers assert, that Nature is unlimited in her operations, that she has inexhaustible treasures in reserve, that knowledge will always be progressive, and that all future generations will continue to make discoveries of which we have not the slightest idea

We are told that matter is indestructible.

15. Nouns of Address and Vocative Expressions.

Nouns of address and vocative expressions should be separated from the rest of the sentence by commas.

Mr. President, I rise to explain.

You talk, sir, of your allies. I wish to know who your allies are.

Let us now, my friends, calmly discuss the matter.

16. Omission of a Noun, a Verb, or a Phrase.

A comma should be used to indicate the omission of a noun, a verb, or a phrase when this mark is necessary to make the meaning clear; in short clauses it may be dispensed with, unless needed to prevent ambiguity.

Reading maketh a full man; conference, a ready man; writing, an exact man.

The young are slaves to novelty; the old to custom

When two short clauses have bearing on a final expression, the comma is omitted after the second clause, and the semicolon before it is changed to a comma.

Herder had more of the Oriental fancy, Schleiermacher more of the European acuteness in his composition.

17. Numbers.

In numbers consisting of four or more figures (except dates), a comma is placed before every three figures beginning at the right.

The population of Chicago in 1900 was 1,698,575.

Numbers expressed in words are usually written without a comma. In expressing round numbers, words are to be preferred to figures.

The population of the United States is about seventy-six millions.

In writing dates a comma should be placed between the month and the year: October 1st, 1899; March, 1900.

18. In the Address and the Conclusion of a Letter
or other document, commas should separate the different items.

Hon. William T. Harris,
    United States Commissioner of Education.
                I remain
                      Yours very respectfully,
                            Howard R. Brown.

In the address on an envelope, no punctuation is needed at the ends of the lines, as they are sufficiently set off by their position.

Commas are needed only where they help to the understanding of the sense. The use or the omission of a comma in a sentence sometimes entirely changes its meaning.

However, this may be.
However this may be.
He who loves the bristle of bayonets, only sees in their glitter what beforehand he felt in his heart.
He who loves the bristle of bayonets only, sees in their glitter what beforehand he felt in his heart.

In cases of doubt, it is best to follow the old rule, and use too few rather than too many commas.

CHAPTER V

THE INTERROGATION POINT—THE EXCLAMATION POINT

THE INTERROGATION POINT

1. Direct Questions.

The interrogation point should be used after every direct question, when an answer is expected or involved.

Will you go to the lecture this evening?
Cans't thou by searching find out God?

It is sometimes difficult to decide whether the interrogation point or the mark of exclamation should be used after a sentence which is interrogative in form. As a general rule, when an answer is expected or implied, the interrogation point should be used; when no answer is either expected or involved, the sentence should be followed by the exclamation point.

What is the happiness that this world can give? Can it defend us from disasters?
How could you desert me!
O Rose! who dares to name thee!

When a rhetorical use is made of a question, it is followed by an interrogation point.

Am I not an apostle? Am I not free?

THE INTERROGATION POINT

2. Questions not Interrogative in Form.

A sentence put in a declarative form but intended as a question, should be followed by an interrogation point.

You will go to the lecture this evening?

3. Sentences Which Denote only that a Question has been asked.

The interrogation point should not be used after a sentence which merely denotes that a question has been asked.

He asked me if I would go to the lecture this evening.
He asked me what I would do in that case.
He was asked the question, Are you guilty or not guilty, and refused to answer.

4. Sentences not Entirely Interrogative.

When a sentence is long and not entirely interrogative, the interrogation point is placed immediately after the interrogative portion.

Shall we blame him?—seeing that he did not know what would be expected of him, and that he would not have understood had he known.

5. A Series of Questions.

The interrogation point is used after each separate query of a compound interrogative sentence.

Does he dream of wealth? or fame? or empire? or happiness?

The members of a compound interrogative sentence are sometimes separated by other points.

Ah! whither now are fled those dreams of greatness; those busy, bustling days; those gay-spent, festive nights; those veering thoughts, lost between good and ill, that shared thy life?

6. Doubt as to the Truth or Accuracy of a Statement.

The interrogation point placed within parentheses is used to question the truth or accuracy of a statement.

Aldus Manutius went to Venice in 1489 (?)

THE EXCLAMATION POINT

1. Interjections, Exclamations, etc.

The exclamation point is used generally after interjections, words used as interjections, exclamations, and phrases or sentences expressing emotion, passion, wish, or wonder. It is not used after sentences which are only slightly exclamatory or which merely express a command, nor is it needed after every *oh* or *alas*.

Ha! that is grand.
No more! Oh, how majestically mournful are those words!—LONGFELLOW.
God save the King!
O blessed vision of the morning, stay!
A wide freedom, truly.
Friends, Romans, countrymen, lend me your ears.

2. Interjections Repeated.

When interjections are repeated to express a certain sound, they are separated from one another by commas and the exclamation point is used only after the last.

Ha, ha, ha! That's the best joke I have heard this many a day.

If an interjection begins a clause or a sentence which requires the exclamation point at the end, it is better to omit the point after the interjection.

Alas both for the deed and for the cause!

3. The Exclamation Point Repeated.

To express strong feeling, the exclamation point is sometimes repeated. It is employed in this way in burlesque and satire, but only to a limited extent.

Fire! Fire!! Fire!!! Dying! Dying!! Dying!!!

O and Oh

O is used with a noun in direct address and to express a wish or imprecation. It is used also to introduce an exclamatory phrase or sentence, and as an introduction to a sentence in which it has no particular meaning.

O thou that rollest above, round as the shield of my fathers!—OSSIAN.

O wad some power the giftie gie us,
To see oursels as ithers see us!—BURNS.

O God! that men should put an enemy in their mouths to steal away their brains!—SHAKESPEARE: *Othello*.

When did you return? O, only yesterday.

O should never be immediately followed by the exclamation point.

In names compounded with o', the *o* should always be a small letter: Tam o'Shanter, five o'clock.

Oh is used to express surprise, pain, or grief. It is followed immediately by the exclamation point, unless used to introduce an exclamatory phrase or sentence, in which case a comma should be used after the interjection and the exclamation point placed at the end. Oh is not used with nouns of address.

Oh! I have lost my purse.

Oh! you are wounded, my lord.

But she is in her grave, and oh!
The difference to me!—WORDSWORTH.

Oh, what a tangled web we weave
When first we practice to deceive!—SCOTT.

CHAPTER VI

THE DASH

1. Change in the Construction or in the Sentiment.

The dash is used to indicate a sudden change in the construction or in the sentiment.

The spectroscope shows the atmosphere of Saturn to be—no matter, I have forgotten what; but it was not pure nitrogen, at any rate.—HOLMES: *Over the Teacups.*

Here lies the great—False marble! where?
Nothing but sordid dust lies here.

The dash is used sometimes to denote hesitation or faltering on the part of the speaker.

I take—eh! oh! as much exercise—eh!—as I can, Madame Gout. You know my sedentary habits.

The dash is used when a sentence takes an unexpected or epigrammatic turn at the end.

Some men are full of affection—affection for themselves.
This world is full of fools, and not to see one pass,
You must shut yourself up alone and—break your
   looking-glass.—LA MONNAYE.

2. Parenthetical Expressions.

The dash is used before and after a parenthetical expression that is too much detached from the sentence to take commas, and yet is too closely related to it to be enclosed within parentheses.

That done, she turned to the old man with a lovely smile upon her face—such, they said, as they had never seen and never could forget—and clung with both her arms about his neck. They did not know that she was dead, at first.—DICKENS.

A comma is used sometimes before the first dash when a comma would be required if the parenthetical expression were omitted. Many writers omit the comma.

And the ear,—that gathers into its hidden chambers all music and gladness—would you give it for a kingdom?

The motive of the play—revenge as a religious duty—belongs only to a social state in which the traditions of barbarism are still operative.

If the parenthetical expression itself requires a point, it should be placed before the last dash.

Religion—who can doubt it?—is the noblest of themes for the exercise of the intellect.

When one parenthetical expression occurs within another, the first parenthetical expression may be separated from the rest of the sentence by marks of parenthesis, and the second set off by dashes.

3. A Series of Clauses Dependent upon a Concluding Clause.

A series of phrases or clauses having a common dependence upon a concluding clause is separated from the latter by a dash.

To pull down the false and to build up the true, and to uphold what there is of true in the old—let this be our endeavor.

In this case some writers use a comma before the dash, but the tendency is to dispense with all unnecessary punctuation.

4. Detached Expressions.

The dash is used when a sentence breaks off abruptly or is apparently completed.

"I forgot my—" "Your portmanteau?" hastily interrupted Thomas. "The same."

He has lost wealth, home, friends—everything but honor.

A whole leisure Saturday afternoon was before him—pure gold without alloy.

5. Repeated Words or Expressions.

The dash is used before words or expressions which are repeated by way of explanation or for the sake of emphasis.

You speak like a boy—like a boy, who thinks the old gnarled oak can be twisted as easily as the young sapling.

Let no sad tears be shed, when I die, over me,
But bury me deep in the sea—in the sea.

6. Ellipses.

The dash is used to indicate the ellipsis of such words as *namely, that is,* etc.

There are two kinds of evils—those which cannot be cured and those which can.

The people of the village thought they recognized in Peter a most illustrious personage—the king of Prussia in disguise.

He has happily united the two most familiar emblems of life—the short journey and the inn.

In such cases, especially in short sentences, many writers use a comma instead of the dash.

7. Sideheads and Extracts.

The period and the dash are used after a sidehead, that is, a heading at the beginning of a paragraph. These marks are placed also after an extract, when the name of the author or work from which the extract is taken follows in the same paragraph. In these cases the dash is an ornamental mark used by the printer.

THE AGE OF ELIZABETH.—Lectures on the History of English Literature, from the Revival of Learning to Milton, exclusive of the Drama.

There is no genius in life like the genius of energy and industry.—D. G. MITCHELL.

8. Change of Subject in the Same Paragraph.

A dash may be used to denote a change of subject in a paragraph, when, from want of space, a separate paragraph cannot be made. It is so employed in dictionaries and encyclopedias Questions and answers when given in the same paragraph are separated by the dash

Where was Napoleon born?—In the island of Corsica. What sobriquet was bestowed upon him in France?—"The Little Corporal."

9. Omission of Letters and Figures.

A long dash is used to indicate the omission of letters from a word, when it is not desirable to give the word in full.

If you have written anything which you think well of, show it to Mr. ——, the well-known critic.

A reception was held last evening at the residence of Mrs. L———, on B——— Street.

A short dash is used to indicate the omission of figures: 1890–91.

When used between two numbers, the dash shows that the numbers given and all the intervening ones are in a series: Pages 339–400 ; Matthew iv: 5-10; St. John v: 1-9.

In writing dates, only the figures denoting the century should be dropped: 1896-97. The full figures should be used in giving pages or numbers.

The dash is a mark which should be used sparingly. It should not be made to take the place of other punctuation marks nor to separate complete sentences. Its frequent use tends to disfigure a page either of manuscript or of printed matter.

CHAPTER VII

MARKS OF PARENTHESIS—BRACKETS

MARKS OF PARENTHESIS

1. Words Which Break the Unity of a Sentence.

Marks of parenthesis are used to enclose words which break the unity of a sentence and which have no necessary connection with the sentence in which they occur.

The profound learning and philosophical researches of Sir William Jones (he was the master of twenty-eight languages) were the wonder and admiration of his contemporaries.

A. B. (*Artium Baccalaureus*) is an abbreviation meaning Bachelor of Arts.

Si monumentum requiris, circumspice (If you seek his monument, look around) is the epitaph of Sir Christopher Wren in St. Paul's Cathedral, London.

2. Punctuation Within a Parenthesis.

Marks of parenthesis do not take the place of other marks of punctuation.

Words enclosed within the parenthesis should be punctuated as independent sentences. A period is sometimes required before the last curve.

Say not in thine heart, Who shall ascend into heaven? (that is, to bring Christ down from above;) or, Who shall descend into the deep? (that is, to bring up Christ again from the dead.) But what saith it?

3. Punctuation Before and After a Parenthesis.

If no mark would be required with the parenthesis omitted, no point should be placed either before the first or after the last curve.

For I know that in me (that is, in my flesh) dwelleth no good thing.—St. Paul.

If a mark is required after the portion of the sentence preceding the parenthesis, it should be placed after the second curve.

I cite this, not that it is the only instance (for there are many others), but because the violation in this particular is too notorious and palpable to be denied.

Just at that moment the candle went out, and the brother-in-law, looking through a chink in the door, saw the two dark men stealing upstairs; one armed with a dagger that long (about five feet); the other carrying a chopper, a sack, and a spade.

When the parenthesis is a question or an exclamation, the comma is placed before the first curve.

While a Christian desires the approbation of his fellow-men, (and why should he not desire it?) he desires to receive their good-will by honorable means.

Let me be understood, however, distinctly as not meaning to say that I dread war in a just cause, (and in no other way may it be the lot of this country ever to engage!) from a distrust of the strength of the country to commence it, or of her resources to maintain it.—George Canning: *Aid to Portugal.*

So far as possible, parentheses should be avoided. In many cases the thought can be conveyed by a different construction of the sentence. The dash, however, should not be used as a cover for ignorance of the proper marks to be employed, nor to set off all kinds of parenthetical expressions.

The parentheses and the dash have their separate offices. An interpolation that has no necessary connection with the sentence in which it occurs and which could be constructed as an independent sentence, should be enclosed within parentheses. The dash serves to indicate a sudden change in the construction or sentiment, or an expansion of the thought already expressed.

BRACKETS

1. Extraneous Matter.

Brackets are used to enclose all extraneous matter, such as interpolations, corrections, criticisms, or explanations, made by an editor, or by a writer in a quotation from another person.

Few books have been perused by me with greater pleasure than his [Watts's] "Improvement of the Mind."—Dr. S. Johnson.

K. C. H., Knight Commander of [the Order of] Hanover.

Let us beseech you, then, to make them [religion and eternity] familiar with your minds and mingle them with the ordinary stream of your thoughts; retiring often from the world, and conversing with God and your own souls.—Robert Hall.

2. Reports of Speeches.

In reports of speeches, names of persons referred to by the writer of the report, and exclamations of approbation and disapprobation, are enclosed within brackets.

In doing so, I agree with my honorable friend [Mr. Canning] that it would, in any case, be impossible to separate the present discussion from the former crimes and atrocities of the French Revolution.

We have met for the freest discussion of these resolutions, and the events which gave rise to them. [Cries of "Question," "Hear him," "Go on," "No gagging," etc.]

3   Interpolation in a Parenthesis.

An interpolation made by the writer in matter already enclosed within marks of parentheses should be placed within brackets.

They have given way to the absolute power of one man, concentrating in himself all the authority of the state, and differing from other monarchs only in this, that (as my honorable friend [Mr. Canning] truly stated it) he wields a sword instead of a sceptre.—WILLIAM PITT: *Refusal to Negotiate.*

4. Printed Dramas.

In printed dramas, brackets are used to enclose stage directions, and, in single form, to indicate the entrance and departure of certain characters.

Shylock. [Aside.] How like a fawning publican he looks!

Lennox. May't please your highness, sit.
  [The ghost of Banquo enters, and sits in
      Macbeth's place.

[Various Women and Bathsheba come slowly on in the
    gallery above.
            [Exit Gadias. Murmurs outside.

Words enclosed within marks of parentheses are a part of the original matter, that is, they are explanations given by the writer or speaker. What is enclosed within brackets is extraneous matter, or the words of the reporter or editor or of some other person than the speaker or writer.

Or, even if the construction contended for is admitted, let us see what would have been its application, let us look at the list of their aggressions which was read by my right honorable friend [Mr. Dundas] near me. With whom have they been at war since the period of this declaration? With all the nations of Europe save two (Sweden and Denmark), and if not with these two, it is only because, with every provocation that could justify defensive war, those countries have hitherto acquiesced in repeated violations of their rights rather than recur to war for their vindication.—WILLIAM PITT: *Refusal to Negotiate.*

CHAPTER VIII

QUOTATION MARKS—THE APOSTROPHE

QUOTATION MARKS

1. Quoted Words or Passages.

Marks of quotation are used to enclose passages from an author or what is said by another person, if given in his own words.

Goethe says, "Man makes mistakes so long as he strives."
When Fenelon's library was on fire, "God be praised," said he, "that it is not the dwelling of a poor man."

When the substance only of a passage is given or when the words of another are not given in the first person, quotation marks should not be used.

Socrates said that he believed in the immortality of the soul.
Swift asserts that no man ever wished himself younger.

When an extract is taken from a work and credit is given to the writer in the text or in a foot-note, quotation marks are superfluous.

2. Quotations Consisting of More than One Paragraph.

When cited matter consists of more than one paragraph, quotation marks are used before each paragraph, but they are not placed at the end of any paragraph except the last.

The following paragraphs are taken from an essay by Godwin:

"No subject is of more importance in the morality of private life than that of domestic or family life

"Every man has his ill-humors, his fits of peevishness and exacerbation. Is it better that he should spend these upon his fellow-beings, or suffer them to subside of themselves?"

If the matter quoted does not begin a new paragraph, no paragraph should be made before the close of the quotation.

D'Alembert congratulated a young man very coldly, who had brought him the solution of a problem. "I have done this to have a seat in the Academy," said the young man. "Sir," answered D'Alembert, "with such motives you will never earn one. Science must be loved for its own sake, and not for the advantage to be derived. No other principle will enable a man to make true progress."

3. A Break in a Quotation.

A break in a quotation is generally indicated by points or periods. No quotation marks are used except at the beginning and the end of the whole matter quoted. If the words following the points begin another paragraph, they should be preceded by quotation marks.

. . . . . "Ah, nothing is too late
Till the tired heart shall cease to palpitate.
Cato learned Greek at eighty.

. . . .

Chaucer, at Woodstock with the nightingales,
At sixty wrote the Canterbury Tales.
Goethe, at Weimar, toiling to the last,
Completed Faust when eighty years were past."

If a dash is used to denote that a quotation is not complete, quotation marks should be placed after the dash.

"O Cæsar, we who are about to die
Salute you! was the gladiator's cry
In the arena——"

4. Use of Quotation Marks in Latin Languages.

In many foreign books, especially in French, Spanish, and Italian novels, no quotation marks are used in dialogues or conversations, a dash serving to indicate the beginning of a conversation, also when one person ceases speaking and another begins. Some publishers use quotation marks, but only at the beginning and the end of the whole dialogue or conversation. Quotation marks are always employed, however, to enclose extracts and short quotations from the words of others.

In the authorized version of the Bible, an initial capital takes the place of an opening quotation mark, yet there is no difficulty in distinguishing the spoken words from the descriptive portion of the text.

The marks now generally used in English to enclose the words of different speakers in dialogues and conversations, therefore, are not really needed. An initial capital at the beginning of the words of each speaker, or a dash and capital if what is said by the various persons forms separate paragraphs, would sufficiently set apart the conversation from the rest of the text. Quotation marks, however, should always be used to enclose the exact words of an author or of a speaker.

5. A Quotation Within a Quotation.

Single marks should be used to enclose a quotation included within another quotation.

A minister of some experience remarks, "I have heard more than one sufferer say, 'I am thankful, God is good to me'; and when I heard that I said 'It is good to be afflicted.'"

In books printed in England, single instead of double marks are placed before and after quoted matter; a quotation included within another is enclosed with double marks.

6. Words Spoken of by Name.

Words spoken of by name are generally enclosed in single quotation marks: the verb 'to do'; the adjective 'beautiful'. Some writers use italic type to specify such words. In long lists no distinguishing mark is considered necessary. The meaning would be quite as clear in any case, if the words were put simply in roman with no enclosing marks.

7. Titles of Books, Periodicals, Pictures, etc.

Quotation marks are used to enclose titles of books, periodicals, plays, pictures, etc.

One of the best known of the works of Dickens is "David Copperfield."

If the title is well known or is used frequently, or if many titles occur in the same work, they should be printed in roman type without quotation marks.

The Iliad, The Æneid; the Messiah, the Creation; the Dance of Death.

Titles of books in foreign languages are put by some authors in italics; when thus printed no quotation marks should be used.

La Mare au Diable; Die Rauber; La Divina Commedia; La Vida es Sueno.

When reference is made to characters found in books or plays, the names are sometimes put in italics. This is necessary only when the name of the character is the same as the title of the work.

Names of vessels, which were once either enclosed in quotation marks or put in italic type, are now printed in roman.

Neither italic letter nor quotation marks are really needed to specify the titles of books and periodicals. In most cases, the titles are sufficiently distinguished by the initial capitals.

8. Position of Points of Punctuation Used With Closing Quotation Marks.

The period and the comma, at the close of a quoted passage, are usually placed by compositors before or rather under the quotation mark, whether they belong only to the quotation or to the sentence as a whole. This is probably done because both these points are so small that they seem isolated when placed outside the closing quotation mark. When a quotation occurs at the end of a sentence but is only a portion of that sentence, the mark needed to punctuate the entire sentence properly belongs after the closing quotation mark. When the quotation forms one complete sentence, the quotation marks, of course, follow the point.

THE APOSTROPHE

The apostrophe is used to denote:

1. The possessive case; as, my brother's house; James's father; children's games.

In order to avoid a prolonged hissing sound, when more than two sounds of *s* would come together the possessive may be formed by the use of the apostrophe only: Moses' hat, Francis' son, for conscience' sake. If the sound of the *s* forming the possessive is not given in pronunciation, the letter is not needed in writing the word.

The possessive case of *it* (its) is written without the apostrophe; the possessive of *one*, with the apostrophe: one's feelings; *but* itself, oneself.

In such titles as *Farmers National Bank, Adams Express Company, Teachers College, Ladies Dressingroom*, some publishers regard the first word of the title as an adjective and write it without the apostrophe; others retain the sign of the possessive case.

2. The intentional elision of a letter or letters; as, I'm for I am; 'tis for it is.

3. The omission of the century in dates, when the century is understood; as, The Fourth of July, '76.

4. The plural of figures and letters: there are three 5's in the number; your *n*'s and *u*'s are made too much alike. In forming the plural of figures, the apostrophe might be altogether omitted. In

making the plural of letters, it is sometimes needed to prevent confusion: *i's* without the apostrophe would be *is*, and *u's* would become *us*. The apostrophe is never needed when the plural of a figure or letter is written in full: there are three *fives* in the number; this line is nineteen *ems* long.

CHAPTER IX

THE HYPHEN

The hyphen is used both to join and to separate. It is employed between the parts of some compound words; also to divide words into syllables, either at the end of a line or for the purpose of showing the proper pronunciation.

Fellow-being, twenty-five, long-suffering, in-dus-tri-ous.

Neither hyphen nor dieresis is needed in such words as:

Coordinate, cooperate, zoology, reestablished, preeminent.

In *re-creation, re-formation* (forming anew), and similar words, the hyphen is used to distinguish the word from another spelled in the same way, but having a different meaning.

Such words as the following are usually written with the hyphen:

Neo-platonism, pre-raphaelite, non-essential, inter-relationship, thermo-electric, a-hunting.

COMPOUND WORDS

A compound word is made up of two or more simple words, each of which is used separately in English; as, eyeball, meeting-house. A derivative contains simple words, and parts of words which are not used separately in English; as, neo-Greek, pseudo-branch.

1. Separate simple words in common use which are accented as single words, should be united without the hyphen:

anybody, everything, anywhere, somewhere, eyebrow, railroad, forevermore.

any one and every one are written as separate words.

2. When only one of two simple words forming a compound is strongly accented, the compound is generally written as one word:

bookseller, blackberry, classroom, copperplate, glassware, grandfather, stepdaughter, needlework, northeast, southwest, schoolfellow, towboat, townfolk, township.

town gate, town hall, town house, and town talk are written as separate words.

3. Attributive adjectives are generally compounded: a high-minded man, a well-ventilated house, the above-named conditions, the so-called reforms.

Such long phrases as the following should not be compounded:

attorney at law, pen and ink (drawing), by and by, ever to be remembered, long looked for, much to be regretted, never to be forgotten, uncalled for, well to do.

4. A compound should not be made when separate words will convey the meaning quite as well:

coffee trade, common school, common sense, multiplication table, sister city, Sunday school, good morning.

5. A compound should not be made simply because a noun is used as an adjective:

brother minister, county town, grand jury, master printer, mountain top, palm leaf, peasant woman, supper table.

6. When either of two nouns in apposition is applicable separately to the person or thing mentioned, the hyphen is not used; when the nouns are not in apposition, and only one is applicable to the person or thing, they are sometimes united by the hyphen.

Lord Chief Justice, Lord Mayor, Major General; *but* field-marshall, bone-setter.

Many words of the latter class have been consolidated: bookkeeper, bookseller, newsboy, newspaper.

7. Numerals compounded of tens and digits are written with a hyphen: twenty-one, seventy-six. Numerals are compounded with various adjectives and nouns: one-sided, three-legged, four-footed, five-story; one-horse chaise, twenty-dollar note.

8. Such fractions as the following, when written out, are made separate words: one half, three quarters, seven eighths, five thousandths. Compounds of *half quarter*, and *eighth*, generally take the hyphen: half-dollar, half-past, half-yearly, quarter-deck, quarter-barrel; *but* halfpenny, headquarters, quartermaster.

9. Compounds ending with *board, boat, book, drop, house, light, room, side, stone, time,* and *yard* are written as single words, if the first part of the compound consists of only one syllable:

blackboard, bulletin-board; sailboat, canal-boat
schoolhouse, dwelling-house; greenroom, dining-room.
churchyard, marble-yard.

Compound nouns ending with *man* or *woman* should be written as one word, unless the word so formed would be too long:

chairman, countryman, horsewoman, needlewoman, oysterman, marketwoman, workingman, Englishman, Frenchwoman; *but* an Americanwoman.

10. A compound beginning with *school* is not generally hyphened, unless formed with a participle:

schoolboy, schoolfellow, schoolhouse, schoolmaster, schoolmate, schoolroom; school board, school children, school committee, school days, school district, school teacher; school-bred, school-teaching

11. A compound consisting of a present participle and a noun or an adjective is generally written with a hyphen: dining-hall, good-looking, printing-office, writing-desk, writing-paper.

12. With few exceptions, words beginning with *self* take the hyphen: self-esteem, self-love, self-sacrifice; *but* selfhood, selfsame, selfish. When *self* is added as a termination to a pronoun, the compound is written as one word: himself, itself, myself, oneself, themselves.

13. When two words, generally expressed as one, are employed in an unusual sense, they should be written as two separate words.

A *blackbird* is a species of oriole; but a crow is a *black bird*.

The coalescence of words often depends upon the length of time they have been in use. While the idea is novel, words are generally kept apart; as, long boat, steam boat, electric fan. When an object or idea has become common, words are usually written as one: longboat, steamboat, railroad.

The use of the hyphen is to some degree a matter of taste. If the meaning of the compound would not be clear if it were written as one word, if the compound is made with an uncommon word, or if there is an awkward joining of letters, the hyphen should be used.

SYLLABICATION

The proper division of words at the end of lines is not considered a matter of primary importance, as is shown by the inconsistencies in our dictionaries and the discrepancies between them. The proof-reader and the compositor, however, must be governed by some general principles, as the transfer of letters or syllables from one line to another sometimes necessitates the respacing of two or three lines.

The usual practice in English is to divide words so as to show, as nearly as possible, their correct pronunciation, some regard being given also to derivation, composition, and meaning.

1. Every vowel or diphthong which is sounded should make a separate syllable:

a-nem-o-ne, con-tem-plate, la-i-ty, re-al, re-ceive, re-en-ter.

2. A short vowel followed by a single consonant or a digraph[1] keeps the consonant or the digraph with

---

[1] *Digraph*, a combination of two letters to represent one sound, as *ch* in church, *ea* in head.

A Trigraph is a combination of three letters to represent one sound, as *tch* in pitch, *eau* in beau.

it, unless in so doing the sound of the consonant would be misrepresented: hab-it, diaph-a-nous, Goth-ic; *but* le-gend.

3. After long vowels and unaccented short ones, the consonant or consonant combination goes with the following syllable: mo-tive, de-press.

4. Two consonants which do not form a digraph, coming between two vowels or a diphthong and a vowel, must be divided:

ab-bey, ac-celerate, ac-cent, con-ver-sion, for-mer, for-tune, gar-den, mil-lion, pas-ture, per-cep-tible, statis-tics, vel-lum.

5. When three or more consonants occur between two vowels, the first of which is short, all the consonants which can be sounded together except the first should be written with the latter syllable:

blas-pheme, dis-tress, elec-trify, in-struc-tress, pam-phlet, ven-triloquist.

6. The division of a compound word on any syllable is allowable, but it is better to make the separation only between the simple words:

heart-broken, self-sacrificing, fellow-creature, tuning-fork.

7. Proper names consisting of only one word should not be divided.

8. In purely English words, the division is made between the primitive and the suffix, even when the vowel of the primitive is long, except when the *e* or the *i* of the suffix is preceded by soft *c* or *g*. A syllable of only two letters, however, should not be

carried over. When the consonant ending of a primitive is doubled, the second consonant goes with the suffix:

bak-ing, lin-ing, mak-ing, self-ish, wis-dom, fast-est, wisest; *but* roman-cer, embra-cing, char-ging; hot-ter, run-ning.

There are but few purely English suffixes. Some of those most commonly used are:

ed, er, en, ing, ish, dom, ship, ful, hood, less, ness, ry, ty, y, ways, wise, and er and est, the signs of the comparative and the superlative degrees of adjectives.

9. In words with Latin or Greek terminations, the division is generally made according to sound:

practi-cal, condo-lence, stu-dent, percep-tive, systematize, proc-tor, opera-tor.

10. *C* or *g* should always be joined to the following *e*, *i*, or *y* which governs its soft sound: ne-cessary, capa-city, le-gend, sur-ging.

11. The letter *x* should never begin a syllable, as no English word begins with it; *j* should never end a syllable, as it never ends an English word: paroxysm, pre-judice.

12. Such terminations as *cial*, *tial*, *sion*, *tion*, etc., which are pronounced as one syllable, should never be divided. The letter *q* should never be separated from the *u* which always follows it in an English word:

artifi-cial, par-tial, provi-sion, posi-tion; li-quid, re-quisition, ubi-quity

13. In cases where the exact pronunciation is doubtful, or where it cannot be indicated, the division should be made upon the vowel:

dou-ble, me-moir, pro-duct, pro-gress, wo-man; busi-ness, colo-nel.

14. A line should not end with the first syllable of a word when it is but a single letter; as, a-broad, a-long. A line should not begin with a syllable of but one letter (as *u* in vac*u*um), unless this immediately follows a primitive (as in profit-*a*-ble), nor should it begin with the last syllable when this consists of only two letters; as, exception-al, happi-er, brave-ly.

Three or more lines in succession should not end with the hyphen. The division of words at the end of a line, whether in print or manuscript, should be made as seldom as possible. The principles of taste and beauty should be considered as well as the proper mode of syllabication.

CHAPTER X

REFERENCE MARKS—MISCELLANEOUS MARKS

REFERENCE MARKS

References are signs, figures, or letters, which refer to matter in the margin or at the foot of the page.

The following marks were formerly employed as references, in the order given:

Asterisk, or Star *	Section §
Obelisk, or Dagger †	Parallel ‖
Double Dagger ‡	Paragraph ¶

Superior figures and letters have taken the place of these marks.

When notes are given in the margin, the figure [1] or the letter [a] should be the first reference mark on every page containing notes. If the notes are at the end of the work, figures and not letters should be used.

When letters are used as superiors, j should be omitted because of its similarity to i.

Accent Marks are placed over words to indicate their pronunciation; they are acute (ʹ), grave (ˋ), and circumflex (ˆ). Accents are also primary, secondary, and double. Only one such mark (ʹ) is commonly used to denote the stress or accent in English, except in works on elocution, in which the three are employed.

The Brace { is used to connect a number of words on lines one below another, with one common term.

Prelude in B minor,
Air in D, } Johann Sebastian Bach.
Bourrée in B minor,

The brace should point toward the one general term.

The *Breve* shows that the vowel over which it is placed is short: răsh, nĕt, hŏt, bŭt.

The *Caret* is used to indicate the omission of a letter or letters, a word or words. It is employed only in manuscript.

   e   is
Wll begun half done.
  ^   ^

The *Cedilla* is a mark resembling a comma, placed under the letter c to show that it has the sound of sharp *s* before *a* and *o* in words adopted from the French: façade, garçon.

Two Commas are used to show that something is understood which was given in the line and word immediately above. Figures and names of persons spelled in the same way should always be repeated.

   Bought:
Dec. 9, 8 yd. broadcloth.
 " 15, 8 " flannel.
William Smith, Chicago.
William Brown,   "

Marks of Ellipsis consist of a long dash or a succession of points or stars. They show the omission of letters in a word, of words in a sentence, or of sentences in a paragraph. Points are preferable to stars.

Truly, Lady Teazle is as censorious as Miss S———— W————.—SHERIDAN.
You would pity . . . the poor soul that shivers Out here at your door in this merciless blast.—HORACE.
In his conception of characters, Sheridan was a wit rather than a humorist. . . . His humor, fine and dry as it was, was the humor of the wit.—BRANDER MATTHEWS.

The Index calls special attention to a passage. N. B. (*nota bene*), meaning "mark well," is often used for the same purpose.

☞ The door of the lecture-room will be closed promptly at eight o'clock.
N. B. No goods exchanged during the holiday season.

Leaders are points or periods employed in tables of contents and in lists of a similar nature, to direct the eye to the matter at the end of the line.

		PAGE
Introduction	. ...	3
Author's Preface	.. ..	9
Dramatis Personæ	....	13

The *Macron* is a short horizontal line placed over a vowel to show that it has the long sound: lāte, mēte, pīne, rōve, ūtilize.

Three Stars (₊*₊) call attention to some special passage.

The *Tilde* is a mark forming part of the letter ñ in Spanish. It indicates the sound of *n* followed by *y* in English: cañón, niño, señorita.

CHAPTER XI

CAPITAL LETTERS

1. Independent Sentences and Lines of Poetry.

The first word of every independent sentence and of every line of poetry should begin with a capital.

Our chief want in life is somebody who shall make us do what we can. This is the service of a friend. With him we are easily great. There is a sublime attraction in him to whatever virtue is in us.—EMERSON: *Considerations by the Way.*

> Howe'er it be, it seems to me,
> 'Tis only noble to be good;
> Kind hearts are more than coronets,
> And simple faith than Norman blood.
> TENNYSON: *Lady Clara Vere de Vere.*

A capital should begin the first word of a sentence given as an example; the first word following an introductory word or clause; and the first word of a series of numbered phrases or clauses, even when the clauses are not separated by periods.

A proverb contains a truth, generally in terse form; as, Wilful waste makes woeful want.

Resolved, That the House adjourn, *sine die.*

The writer asserts:
(1) That Nature is unlimited in her operations; (2) That she has inexhaustible treasures in reserve; and (3) That all future generations will continue to make discoveries.

2. Direct Quotations and Direct Questions.

Direct quotations, except single words, and direct questions should begin with capitals.

Theodore Parker said that democracy meant, not "I'm as good as you are," but "You're as good as I am."

Maury asks, "What is this you call eloquence?"

3. Proper Nouns and Words Derived from Proper Nouns.

Every proper noun should begin with a capital. Verbs and adjectives derived from proper nouns should be capitalized, unless usage has sanctioned a small letter.

Europe, America; Philip, Zenobia, James, Elizabeth; the Pyrenees, the Strait of Gibraltar, the North Sea.

Roman, American, Elizabethan, Augustan.

romanized, anglicized, americanized, frenchified, italicize.

China, *chinaware;* Cordova, *cordovan* leather; Damascus, *damask;* Philip, *philippics;* Vandal, *vandalism;* Don Quixote, *quixotic.*

Such verbs as *christianize* and *judaize* are now written with a small letter.

4. The Pronoun I and the Interjection O.

The pronoun *I* and the interjection *O* should always be capitals. *Oh* should not be capitalized unless it begins a sentence, a direct quotation, or a line of poetry. (See O AND OH, page 117.)

5. Names of Days, Months, Seasons, and Festivals.

Names of the days of the week, of the months of the year, and of festivals should begin with capitals. The names of the seasons, unless personified, begin with small letters.

Sunday, January, Easter, Thanksgiving.
He will be absent during the summer.

Sunday always begins with a capital; while sabbath, or sabbath-day, is generally written with a small letter.

The words *day*, *holiday*, etc., even when used with a proper name, generally begin with small letters: Christmas day, the Easter holidays.

6. Geographical Names.

General names, such as *county* and *state*, when preceding a specific name, in ordinary writing begin with a small letter: the county of Cumberland, the state of Ohio. In formal writing, both the general name and the specific name begin with capitals. Each name is capitalized also in an appellation bestowed upon a state or city: the Keystone State, the Lone Star State, the Crescent City.

When state means a political community or the powers exercised by government, it begins with a small letter: the states of Europe, the union of church and state.

General names, when not forming part of a proper name, should always begin with a small letter: the law of the state; the exports of this city.

Government is capitalized when it forms part of a proper name: the French Government; *but* the government of the country.

According to the latest usage, and in conformity with the rule for the use of general and specific names, when *river, valley, city, square, street,* or *place* is used with a proper name, the general name is begun with a small letter: the Connecticut river, the river Charles, the Mississippi valley, the city of New York, Union square, York street, Graver's lane, Delancey place. Many writers, however, still use a capital.

When forming part of a proper name, *mountain, lake, province,* and *district* usually begin with capitals.

The Rocky Mountains, the Great Lakes, the Province of Quebec, District of Columbia.

In display matter, both the general and the specific name should be capitalized.

The words *north, east, south,* and *west,* when used to indicate certain sections of a country should be capitalized; when they refer in a general way to a region, or simply denote direction, they are written with a small letter.

The new Northwest. In Southern Europe. The east of Asia.

The dweller on the Pacific Coast regards everything east of the Rocky Mountains as "the East."

They have had snow in the north.

The sun sets in the west. The West is rapidly developing.

7. Names of Important Historic Days, Events, or Documents; of Religious Sects, Political Parties, etc.

Words denoting historic days or events, important documents, and names of bodies of men, religious sects, and political parties, are capitalized.

The Fourth of July; the Ascension; the Constitution, Magna Charta, the Pandects of Justinian; the Pilgrim Fathers; Jew, Protestant, Presbyterian; Republican, Democrat, Conservative, Liberal, the Right, the Left.

Certain epochs and eras that are not derived from proper names, are written with small letters.

The dark age, the middle age; the Augustan age, the Elizabethan age, the Christian era; *but* the Deluge the Captivity, the Advent.

a.m. and *p.m.* are not capitalized in ordinary text matter.

8. Titles of Respect, Affection, Dignity, or Office.

Titles of respect, honor, or affection, and titles of dignity or office, if applied to a particular person or if used in connection with a proper noun or in formal address, should begin with capitals.

Father Ambrosius; Uncle William; the Iron Chancellor.

The President of the United States; the Queen of Spain; Governor Morton.

Her Royal Highness; to His Excellency, the Governor.

When a title used alone is intended as the synonym of a particular person, it is generally capitalized: the President, the Czar, the Sultan, the Pope. When not used as the appellation of a specified person, a title begins with a small letter: he was arrested by a constable.

When such titles as king, duke, general, etc., are used frequently and are not followed by the name of a person, they are not capitalized.

In a title consisting of separate words used with a name, both words in the title should begin with capitals: Major General Greene; Chief Justice Patterson.

In a compound title only one capital is needed: Vice-president Hobart; Ex-president Cleveland. Ex-president used without a proper name, except at the beginning of a sentence, takes small letters: only one ex-president of the United States is now living.

In salutations of letters, only words referring to the person should be capitalized: Dear Friend, My dear Friend, My darling Child.

Von, de, etc., are capitalized only when not preceded by a title or a Christian name: De Quincey, Thomas de Quincey; Van der Linde, Doctor van der Linde.[1]

Words denoting family relations begin with capitals, when used without a possessive pronoun: I received a message from Father; or, I received a message from my father.

Jr. and *sr.* need not be capitalized in ordinary text-matter. In display work they require capitals.

9. Names of the Deity and of Christ.

All names of the Deity and expressions which are titles of the Deity should begin with capitals. Pronouns referring to God or Christ should be capitalized only when used in direct address without a noun,

---

[1] Some writers follow the Continental method and begin these prefixes always with a small letter This, however, is contrary to the established custom of writing English.

or when other pronouns are employed and a capital is needed to prevent confusion.

Jehovah, Creator, Providence, Almighty, the Most High, the Supreme Being.

The Messiah, the Anointed, the Redeemer, Prophet, Master.

These are thy glorious works, Parent of good.

Almighty! thine this universal frame.

Heaven and *Providence,* meaning the Supreme Being, are capitalized. In all other cases, they should begin with small letters.

May Heaven Forbid!

      Above
Live the great gods in heaven and see
What things shall be.—*Swinburne.*

The world was all before them, where to choose
Their place of rest, and Providence their guide.
      MILTON: *Paradise Lost.*

A remarkable providence appeared in the case.

Heathen, pagan, hell, purgatory, and *paradise* begin with small letters. Poetical names, such as Hades, Elysian Fields, take capitals.

10. Names Referring to the Bible.

Names which indicate the Bible or a book or a portion of the Bible should be capitalized.

The Scriptures, the Old Testament, the Gospels, the Epistles, the Revelation of St. John the Divine; King James's Bible, the Mazarin Bible.

Bible meaning simply a book and not *the* book, should begin with a small letter.

This bible is a great typographical curiosity. Many bibles were distributed in that section of the city.

11. Names of Committees, Clubs, Associations, and of Organizations.

Names of committees, clubs, associations, and of organizations, generally, should be capitalized. When the article *the* forms part of an official title or the title of a book, it should begin with a capital, even when it occurs in the middle of a sentence. When the name of a magazine or newspaper is given in the text, the article takes a small letter.

The Committee of One Hundred, Young Men's Christian Association, The Union League, The Right of Way. The matter was noticed in the Telegraph.

12. Advertisements, Cards, etc.

In advertisements, cards, programs, etc., the most important words are generally capitalized, but for this purpose capitals should not be too freely used, or the intended emphasis will not be conveyed.

13. Works on Botany and Zoology.

In works on botany and zoology, names of classes, families, and genera are begun with capitals. The names of species are begun with small letters, unless derived from proper nouns. Specific names occurring in a roman sentence are printed in italics.

14. Titles of Books, Newspapers, Pictures, etc.

In titles all important words, that is, nouns, pronouns, adjectives, verbs, and adverbs, are generally capitalized. This practice is by no means uniform; some writers capitalize only nouns and verbs, others even prepositions when they are long. In some publications only the first word of the title is begun with a capital, this is the foreign method and the method adopted for catalogues by the American Library Association.

The tendency at the present day is to limit so far as possible the number of capitals employed.

CHAPTER XII

THE ITALIC LETTER

ITALIC type is a letter which inclines to the right. It was introduced by Aldus Manutius, a celebrated printer of Venice, who desired a compact type for the purpose of issuing small editions of the classics. The letter was cut by Francisco da Bologna, an able engraver. It is supposed to be copied from the handwriting of Petrarch. An edition of Vergil was put in this letter by Aldus in 1501; an edition of Petrarch, which Aldus issued the same year, is said to be the first Italian work printed in italic type. Originally, this letter was known as Venetian or Aldine; but later it was called italic, except in Germany and Holland, where it received the name of cursiv.

Italic letter was at first intended and was employed for the whole text of classical works, but after a time its use was restricted to portions of a book not properly belonging to the work, such as prefaces, introductions, notes, and indexes, the text being printed in roman; at a later period quotations occurring in the text were put in italic type. All proper names and nearly all words of more than usual significance were at one time printed in this character. At the present day, its chief use is to denote emphasis. For this purpose it should be used sparingly and might altogether be dispensed with; when introduced too frequently it tends to perplex rather than to assist the reader. No italic is used in the Bible, except to show that words not found in the original have been supplied by the translator to make the sense more perfect, yet it is not difficult to tell just where the emphasis should be placed.

At the present day, italic is generally employed, as follows:

1. Unfamiliar words from foreign languages when printed with our alphabet are italicized the first time they appear; roman type is employed for the repetition of these words.

Foreign words which have become familiar through constant use and which are found in the standard English dictionaries should be put in roman type; as, cicerone, dilettante, role, vice versa.

When citations are made from other languages, it is better to use quotation marks and print in roman.

Words spoken of by name should be put in roman, with single quotation marks.

2. The titles of books, pictures, etc., are sometimes put in italic, but roman type with quotation marks is more common.

Titles of books in foreign languages may be put in italics if not quoted.

Neither quotation marks nor italics should be used for titles of well-known works: The Iliad, Faust, The Divine Comedy, Paradise Lost.

3. It is a common practice to print in italic the names of newspapers and magazines, when used

in the body of a book or pamphlet. The titles of periodicals and serials occurring in the text or in a foot-note need no other distinguishing mark than the initial capitals of roman type.

When the name of an author or of a book is put as a credit at the end of a paragraph, roman is used for author and italic for book or periodical.

4. The scientific names of plants and animals, when first used, are put in italic. The name of the species should always be italic, however often it may occur. When other scientific names in botany or zoology are repeated, they are printed in roman.

5. Italic is used for running headlines, headings of tables, sub-headings, and sideheads.

6. In algebraic and other mathematical works, letters used as signs should be printed in italic, whether capital or small.

7. In lists, as in programs, when the enumeration is made by letters instead of figures, the letters should be italics.

In manuscript, italic is indicated by one stroke under the word.

The common Latin abbreviations, i. e., e. g., etc., viz., are usually printed in roman letter.

ALPHABETS, ACCENTS, DIACRITICAL MARKS AND DIVISIONS

IN THE PRINCIPAL MODERN LANGUAGES—ENGLISH, FRENCH, GERMAN, SPANISH, AND ITALIAN

CHAPTER I

DIACRITICAL MARKS

A DIACRITICAL MARK is a point, line, or other sign, added or put near a letter or character, to distinguish it in some way. Diacritical marks are not often used in English, except in schemes of pronunciation in dictionaries; but they form part of the alphabet systems of many languages. These marks are employed for the following purposes:

1. To give a letter a certain phonetic value. The marks attached to the vowels *a, e, o,* in dictionaries are diacritics· fāte, făt; mēte, mĕt; hōly, hŏlly.

2. To denote some particular accent, tone, stress, or emphasis in the transliteration into roman letter of languages having a different alphabet. Such marks are generally used when words from the Russian or the oriental languages are put in our alphabet, but marks so employed convey no fixed meaning to an English reader.

The dieresis is employed in some proper names taken from the German: Göthe, Müller.

In some words adopted from foreign languages, and which are found in the standard English dictionaries, a distinguishing mark is retained: façade, garçon, from the French; cañon, from the Spanish.

3. To distinguish a letter or sign from another of similar form. In German script the letter *u* is written with a curved line over it, to distinguish it from the letter *n* which has the same form.

4. In some languages a diacritical accent mark is used to distinguish a word from another spelled in the same way but having a different meaning: French —où, where, when; ou, or. Spanish—él, he; el, the. Italian—dì, day; di, of, from, or to.

ENGLISH

The hyphen and the apostrophe (formerly the dieresis) are the only orthographical marks which are regularly used in English. The dieresis was formerly used to show that of two vowels which might be given but one sound, each was to be pronounced separately. Words containing such vowels are now written without a distinguishing mark: zoology, cooperate, coordinate, preeminent, reenter. [For Compound Words and Syllabication see HYPHEN, page 136].

CHAPTER II

FRENCH

THE French alphabet has the same letters, with the same roman forms, as the English alphabet; *k* and *w* are not strictly French letters, but are used in words derived from foreign languages.

The following orthographical marks are used:
The acute accent (´) *été*.
The grave accent (`) *mère*.
The circumflex accent (^) *tête*.
The cedilla (,) *façon*.
The dieresis (..) *haïr*.
The apostrophe (') *j'ai*.
The hyphen (-) *y a-t-il*.

The Acute Accent

The acute accent is used only over *e* and denotes the sound of *a* in the English word *day*: *écu, répondre, précédé*. If two *e*'s come together, the first only is made acute: *armée, relevée*.

The Grave Accent

The grave accent is used over *e*, *a*, and *u*; *e* with the grave accent has the sound of *e* in *ell*: *très, pièce*. Certain syllables ending with two *e*'s separated by one or more consonants frequently take the grave accent over the first *e*: *la misère, restèrent*. This, however, is not a general rule, as the accent may be acute or circumflex. The grave accent occurs over *a* in such words as *voilà, holà, déjà, çà, deçà,* and over *a, e,* and *u* in certain words to distinguish them from others of similar spelling: *à*, to, at, in, or with—*a*, has; *là*, there—la, the; *dès*, from, as soon as—*des*, of the, the; *où*, where, when—*ou*, or.

The Circumflex Accent

The circumflex accent is used over the five vowels *a, e, i, o, u.* The vowel is then long in quantity: *âpre, bête, maître, contrôle, sûr.* The circumflex accent shows that a letter (usually *s*) formerly used in the spelling of a word is now omitted: *côte (coste)*, coast; *fête (feste)*, festival.

The Cedilla

The cedilla is placed under *c* when used before *a, o,* or *u,* and gives the letter the sound of sharp *s: ça, François, reçu.*

The Dieresis

The dieresis, or tréma, is placed over the latter of two vowels coming together when they are to be pronounced separately: *haïr,* héroïque.

The Apostrophe

The apostrophe shows the elision of one vowel before another or before silent *h: l'an* for *le an; c'est* for *ce est; s'il* for *si il; l'homme* for *le homme.*

The Hyphen

The hyphen is used:

1. To connect the parts of a compound word: *demi-heure*, half-hour.

2. Between a pronoun and a verb when the pronoun comes last: *avez-vous?* have you? *donnez-moi*, give me; *dormaient-ils?* were they sleeping?

3. Before and after *t* inserted for euphony between a verb ending with a vowel and a pronoun: *va-t-il; pensa-t-il.*

4. Between a word and *ci* or *là* joined to it: *ce temps-ci, ce temps-là, ceux-ci, ci-inclus.*

Capitals

Proper nouns are the only words written with capitals, except at the beginning of a sentence or quotation. Adjectives denoting nationality take a small letter: *américain, français, gothique, latin, parisien.*

The pronoun *je* (I), except at the beginning of a sentence or quotation, is written with a small letter.

The common titles of respect which correspond to Mrs. and Miss in English are sometimes expressed by a capital and superior letters without the period: Mme or *Mme*, Mlle or *Mlle*.

First, second, third, etc., are indicated by 1er, 2me, 3me, or I, II, III. (*premier, deuxième, troisième*). These abbreviations are printed also in small capitals.

Quotation Marks

The *guillemet*, or quotation mark, for extracts from authors or other quoted matter, is used as in

English. In some books no quotation marks are used in dialogues or conversations, a dash serving to indicate the beginning of a conversation, also when one person ceases speaking and another begins. Some publishers use quotation marks, but only at the beginning and the end of the whole dialogue or conversation.

SYLLABICATION

1. A single consonant between two vowels goes with the vowel following: *ca-lèche, dé-part.*

2. As many consonants as can be pronounced together go with the vowel following: *li-braire, re-gret, four-chette, a-pos-trophe.*

3. A division cannot be made upon a single letter, even if joined to an article or other word: *l'édu-cation.*

4. A mute syllable must not be carried over.

5. Compounds are divided upon the originals: *demi-lune, feld-maréchal.*

6. A small word which is part of a compound must not be carried over: *prenez-le, celui-ci, ceux-là.*

7. Divisions are not allowable between two vowels, except after a word or prefix which may be used separately: *anti-orléaniste, extra-ordinaire.*

8. A letter used as a euphonic must always be carried over to the next line.

9. Three divisions in three successive lines are not allowable.

In writing titles an English noun should not be used with a French preposition. Either Comte d'Artois or Count of Artois, but not Count d'Artois; Duc d' Enghien or Duke of Enghien, but not Duke d'Enghien.

CHAPTER III

GERMAN

THE German alphabet has the same twenty-six letters as the English.

German Alphabet

Aa, Bb, Cc, Dd, Ee, Ff, Gg, Hh, Ii, Jj, Kk, Ll, Mm, Nn, Oo, Pp, Qq, Rr, Sſs, Tt, Uu, Vv, Ww, Xx, Yy, Zz.

Modified vowels, ä, ö, ü.
Combination of Letters:
  Double vowels, aa, ee, oo.
  Diphthongs, ai, au, äu, ei, eu.
  Compound Consonants, ch, ck, ng, pf, ph, qu, sch, sp, st, sz, th, tz.

The short s is used only at the end of a word or syllable; the long s (ſ) at the beginning and in the middle of a word. ss (ſſ) is employed only in the middle of a word, between two short vowels: Küſſe, Waſſer.

The modified vowels, both small and capital, are now written only with the sign (″) placed over the vowel. In some proper names of persons, the double vowel form is still used: Goethe. Such names are written also with the modified vowel: Göthe.

The German has no accent marks.

German Forms

ä, ö, and ü are represented in the roman alphabet by a, o, and u. The diphthongs æ and œ should never be used for ä and ö.

e and i never have the umlaut.

The plural of many nouns is made by simply modifying the vowel: Garten, Gärten; Vater, Väter.

In German script the small u is always written with a curved line over it: ū

Y (ipsilon) is not strictly a German letter and is rarely used.

The German printed characters for the capital letters I and J (ℑ) are the same.

Care is needed not to confound the following letters when printed in German type:

b (b) and h (h); f (f) and ſ (s); r (r) and x (x); v (v), p(p), and y (y) B (B) and V (V); C (C) and E (E); D (D), O (O), and Q (Q); G (G) and S (S); K (K), N (N), and R (R); M (M) and W (W).

Capitals

The following words are begun with capitals:

1. All substantives and words used as substantives: der Tisch, das Singen.

2. The personal pronouns: Sie (you), Ihnen (to you), Ihr (you), Du (thou), Dir (to thee), Dein (thine), Euch (you), in letters; Du and Dein in addressing God. Ich (I), except at the beginning of a sentence or a quotation, takes a small letter.

3. Words in apposition with proper names: Friedrich der Grosse.

4. Adjectives formed from the names of persons and places: die Kantische Philosophie; die Berliner Kinder. Adjectives formed from the names of countries and peoples begin with small letters: die amerikanischen Nationen; die romische Kirche.

An effort is being made by many authors and publishers to limit the use of initial capitals.

The Apostrophe

The apostrophe is used in certain words to indicate the omission of one vowel before another: ich lieb' dich; das leid' ich nicht; heil'ge. Certain words are frequently joined in colloquial speech: ist's? (is it?), geht's? (does it go?)

When a preposition is consolidated with an article, the apostrophe is not used: beim, zum.

If a proper name in the genitive ends with a letter which easily takes an *s* after it, the apostrophe is omitted: Schillers Gedichte. If an *s* would not easily coalesce with the last letter, the apostrophe only is used: Demosthenes' Reden.

Quotations

In printed matter, two sharp-pointed commas are placed before the bottom of the letter beginning the quotation; the same marks upsidedown are used at the close: „Blicke vorwärts! bereite dich zu handeln." Apostrophes are not used to enclose quotations.

Syllabication

1. Compound words are divided according to their components: Staats-Zeitung

2. A consonant between two vowels goes with the latter vowel: Freu-de; lei-den.

3. Any combination of consonants, except ch, ph, sch, th, and dt when it forms only one sound, may be separated: Ach-sel, bes-ser, Freun-de, hin-ter, Knos-pe, krat-zen; *but* Sta-dte.

4. If more than two consonants come together in the middle of a word, the last goes with the following syllable: Gesich-tes. *st* after a preceding consonant, and *sch* after a preceding *r* or *m* are carried to the following syllable: er-ste, Bur-schen.

In dropping the article in author entries and titles used in catalogues or other alphabetical lists, care should be taken to preserve in the singular the nominative form of adjectives, as in German the case is shown partly by the termination of the word, and these terminations are sometimes modified by the article: der deutsche Verein, deutsch*er* Verein, ein deutsch*er* Verein.

CHAPTER IV
SPANISH

The Spanish alphabet contains twenty-nine letters. *ch*, *ll*, and *rr* are compound letters, but in their written and printed forms are considered simple consonants. *w* is employed only in words taken from foreign languages; the use of *k* is restricted also to such words.

The following roman forms are employed:

a, b, c, ch, d, e, f, g, h, i, j, k, l, ll, m, n, ñ, o, p, q, r, rr, s, t, u, v, x, y, z.

ACCENTS

The acute is the only accent mark employed in Spanish.

Rules governing the written accent:

1. Words ending in a vowel, or in *n* or *s*, which in speaking are accented on the last syllable, take the accent mark on that syllable: *café, está, vendrá, renglón, después*.

2. Words ending in a vowel, or in *n* or *s*, which are accented on the syllable next to the last take no accent mark: *toma, margen, crisis*.

3. Words ending in any consonant except *n* or *s*, and which are accented on the last syllable, take no accent mark: *alud, esperar, peral*.

4. Words ending in a consonant other than *n* or *s*, and which are accented on the syllable next to the last, take the accent mark: *ángel, azúcar, clímax, lápiz*.

5. Words accented on a syllable before the penultimate take the accent mark: *músico, atmósfera, paseábamos.*

The accent mark is employed also in Spanish:

1. To distinguish a word from another of similar spelling, but having a different meaning.

bajó, I descend.   *bajo,* low, below.
cómo, I eat.   *como,* as
dé, give (sub. pres. of dar). *de,* of, from.
él, he   *el,* the.
está, he, she, or it, is.   *esta,* this.
éste, this one.   *este,* this.
sé, I know; be thou.   *se,* oneself.
són, sound.   *son,* are.

2. Over the preposition *á,* the conjunctions *é, ó, ú,* and the adverb *aun* when it follows the verb to which it belongs

¿Aun no ha partido? No ha partido aún.

3. Over pronouns and adverbs used interrogatively or exclamatorily, or when repeated as correlatives.

cómo, how?   *como,* as.
cúyo, whose?   *cuyo,* whose.
dónde, where?   *donde,* where.
quién, who? whom?   *quien,* who, whom.

Cuándo de una manera, *cuándo* de otra; *cuáles* hablaban, *cuáles* cantaban

4. Over the weak vowel of a diphthong or triphthong, or over the first if both vowels of a diphthong are weak, to show that the vowels make two syllables: *continúan, creído, decíais, días, flúido, increíble, paraíso, período, poesía.*

a, o, e are the strong vowels; *i* and *u* the weak vowels.

If the written accent is required over a diphthong or triphthong, it is placed over the strong vowel, or, if both vowels of a diphthong are weak, over the last vowel. The diphthong or triphthong is not thereby dissolved; the accent mark indicates where the stress of voice should fall: *parabién, huérfano, seguí, estudiáis.*

5. Over the aorist form of a verb which is accented on the final syllable: *fuí, leí, rió, seguí.*

The tense of a verb requiring the written accent retains it when one or more pronouns are added to it: *diómelos, rióse.*

When the addition of the pronouns places the accent nearer the beginning than the penultimate, the accent must be indicated: *enviándomelos, dándoselos.*

u after a *g* coming before *e* and *i* is silent, and the *g* then has the same sound as in the English word *go· águila, guerra.* When the *u* is to be sounded, the dieresis must be placed over it: *agüero, argüir.*

The mark in *ñ* is called *tilde* and must never be omitted from the letter.

An inverted interrogation or exclamation point is placed at the beginning of a sentence or clause which is interrogative or exclamatory, in addition to the mark at the end. The inverted point may be omitted at the beginning of a sentence when the first word indicates the interrogation or exclamation, as the accent placed over the word shows the nature of the sentence or clause: *Cómo está usted?* How are you?

In Spanish no adjective is written with a capital, except in titles or at the beginning of a sentence: *americano, madrileño.* When adjectives derived from proper nouns are used as substantives they begin with capitals: *los Americanos, los Madrileños.*

The pronoun *yo* (I), except at the beginning of a sentence or quotation, is written with a small letter.

Quotation Marks

Double quotation marks (*comillas*) are used in Spanish, but mainly for the purpose of enclosing extracts or short quotations from the words of others. They are usually repeated at the beginning of each line of the quoted matter. For dialogues, quotation marks are not used, but a dash is placed at the beginning of each paragraph. A break or interruption in conversational matter is indicated by *puntos suspensivos* (. . .).

Syllabication

In dividing a word into syllables, the syllable should end, if possible, in a vowel.

1. A single consonant between two vowels goes with the following vowel: ca-ño, có-mi-co, fa-ci-li-dad, flu-xión. A prepositional prefix should form a separate syllable: a-for-tu-na-do, *des*-a-for-tu-na-do.

2. *ch, ll,* and *rr* are considered simple consonants, and must not be separated: *ca-chu-cha, be-llo-ta, pe-rro.* ñ is joined to the vowel which follows it: *le-ña.*

3. When a syllable consists of but one vowel it should not be written alone, either at the end or the

beginning of a line: *oca-sión*, not *o-casión; arra-bal*, not *a-rrabal*.

The division of words of four letters is not allowable except in very narrow pages or columns. Not more than three divisions should be made in consecutive lines.

CHAPTER V

ITALIAN

THE Italian alphabet contains twenty-two letters. It is the same as the English, with the omission of *k, w, x,* and *y.*

THE WRITTEN ACCENT

There are three written accents in Italian—the *grave,* the *acute,* and the *circumflex.*

The grave is the only accent regularly used. Italian writers and publishers do not entirely agree as to the use of any of the accent marks.

The grave accent occurs regularly only over the last syllable of words. It is always placed on the last letter, as follows:

1. On the last syllable of a word ending with a vowel, when the stress in pronunciation falls on this syllable: *città, portò*

2. On the last vowel of monosyllables which end with a diphthong: *già, più.*

3. On certain monosyllables to distinguish them from others of similar spelling but of different signification: è, is—*e,* and; dì, day—di, of, from, or to.

4. On the last vowel of a shortened form of the preterite, to distinguish it from the present infinitive of the same verb: amàr—amarono; amar—amare.

5. The grave accent is placed over *i* in the terminations *ia* and *io* to show that these letters form two distinct syllables: *cavallerìa, addìo*.

The acute accent is sometimes used over such terminations, but the grave is preferable.

The circumflex is sometimes employed over certain shortened forms of words to distinguish them from other words of similar spelling, but with a different meaning: *côrre* (*cogliere*) to take, to gather; *corre*, he [or she] runs.

The Apostrophe

The apostrophe is used to show the elision of the final vowel of an article coming before a word beginning with a vowel: *l'amore, l'isola, un'altro*.

The apostrophe is used also to denote an abbreviation or contraction: *de'piedi, coll'uomo, dov'è, nient' altro, anch'io, Lorenzo de' Medici*.

j is only another way of writing *i*. In some modern Italian books it is not used.

Syllabication

In Italian, words are so divided that, if possible, every syllable shall begin with a consonant: *fra-tel-lo, ta-vo-la, fir-ma, sem-pre*.

All consonants which can be pronounced together go with the vowel following them.

INDEX

Abbreviated words, how punctuated, 94
Accent, the acute:
    in French, 161
    in Spanish, 169
    the circumflex, in French, 162
    the grave:
        in French, 161
        in Italian, 174
Accent marks, 144
Adams, Joseph A., 83
Adverbs and adverbial phrases, 110
Aldus Manutius, 156
American Library Association, method of capitalization adopted by, 155
American Type-Founders Association, 27
American Type-FoundersCompany, 21
Antique Type, definition of, 66
    specimen of, 33
Apostrophe, the uses of the:
    in English, 134
    in French, 162
    in German, 167
    in Italian, 175
Appleton and Company, D., 38
Apposition, words or phrases in, 106
    statements in, 98

Barth, Henry, 25

Bible, use of capitals for names referring to, 153
Bible text, 30
Binney and Ronaldson, 21
Black letter, definition of, 66
    specimen of, 33
Body of type, 23, 26, 66
Bold-face type, definition of, 66
    specimen of, 33
Brace, the, 145
Brackets, the uses of, 126
Breve, the, 145
Brochure, definition of, 67
Brown Paper Company, L. L., 55
Bruce, David, 82
Bruce, David, jr., 21
Bruce, D. and G., 21
Bruce, George, 27, 30 *note*

Capital letters, the uses of:
    in English, 147
    in French, 163
    in German, 166
Capitals, definition of, 67
Cards, capitals employed for, 154
    how punctuated, 96
Caret, the, 145
Case, definition of, 67
    lower, 34, 74
    upper, 34, 80
Caslon, William, 20

Casting type:
    by hand, 25
    by machinery, 24
    number cast in a minute, 25
Cedilla, the, 145
    in French, 162
Chase, definition of, 67
Church, Dr. William, 35
Church text, specimen of, 33
Cicero, name of type, 30 *note*, 31
Clarendon type, specimen of, 33
Clauses, how punctuated·
    correlative, 106
    explanatory, 101
    having dependence upon another clause, 101, 120
    parenthetical, 108
    relative, 109
    transposed, 107
Colon, the uses of the, 97
Colophon, definition of, 67
Comma, the uses of the, 103
Commas, Two, 145
Composing, definition of, 67
Composing stick, 34, 67
Compound words, 136
Condensed type, definition of, 67
    specimen of, 29
Contrast, words or phrases in, 106
Copy, definition of, 67
    directions for preparing, 10
Corrections:
    cost of author's, 18
    how to make, on proof-sheet, 14
Counter-punch, 21, 22
Cut-in letter, definition of, 67
Cut-in note, definition of, 68

Cylinder machine, 46, 52

Daily Graphic, The, 86 *note*
Dash, the uses of the, 119
Deity and Christ, capitals for names referring to the, 152
Diacritical marks, 159
Didot, François Ambroise, 27
Didot, Henri, 32
Didot, the Messrs., 46
Dieresis, the:
    in English, 136, 160
    in French, 162
Displayed, definition of, 68
Distribute, definition of, 68
Doric type, specimen of, 33
Doubling of points, 94
Dummy, definition of, 68
Duodecimo, definition of, 68

Eighteen-point (great primer) type, 29
Eight-point (brevier) type, 28, 32
Electrotyping, 81, 83
Eleven-point (small pica) type, 28, 31
Ellipsis, marks of, 145
Elzevir old-style type, specimen of, 33
Em, definition of, 69
English, orthographical marks used in, 160
Envelope, address on, 113
Errors, detecting, 16
    which escape notice, 16
Esparto, 46 *note*, 48
Essonnes paper-mills, 46

Even pages, definition of, 69
Exclamation point, the uses of the, 116
Expanded type, 69
Extended type, 29, 69
Extra-condensed type, 29, 67

Five and one-half point (agate) type, 32
Five-point (pearl) type, 32
Folding sheets of paper for binding, 60
Folio, definition of, 60, 69
Font of type, what it comprises, 69
Form of type, 70
Forwarding, definition of, 69
Four and one-half point (diamond) type, 32
Fourdrinier machine, 46, 51
Fourdrinier, the Messrs., 46
Fournier, Pierre Simon, 27
Four-point (brilliant) type, 32
Fourteen-point (English) type, 30
Francisco da Bologna, 156
Frank Leslie's, 86 *note*
Franklin, Benjamin, 21
French:
    alphabet, 161
    orthographical marks used in, 161
Frisket, definition of, 70
Fudge, definition of, 70
Furniture, definition of, 70

Gaillarde type, 31
Galley, 34, 70

Galley proof, 70
Garamond, Claude, 20
Ged, William, 81
Genoux of France, 82
Geographical names, capitals used for, 149
German alphabet, 165
German text, 66, 70
    specimen of, 33
Gilpin, Thomas, 46
Gleason's Pictorial, 86 *note*
Gothic letter, 33, 66, 71, 78
Gothic type, specimen of, 33
Gros romain type, 30

Half-tones, 86, 87, 89
Harper and Brothers, 38
Harper's Weekly, 86 *note*
Headings, how punctuated, 96
Hyphen, the uses of the:
    in English, 136, 160
    in French, 163

I and O, 148
Index, the, 146
Illustrated London News, The, 86 *note*
Imposing, definition of, 71
Imposing stone, definition of, 71
Imprint, definition of, 72
Indention, definition of, 72
Infinitive phrases, 110
Inset, 63, 72
Interrogation point, the uses of the 114
Italian alphabet, 174

Italic letter, definition of, 72
    how employed, 156
Italic type, specimen of, 33

Jenson, Nicolas, 78
Job-work, 42, 72
Johnson Foundry, 21
Johnson, William M., 21
Jungfer type, 32
Justifying, 34, 72

Kerned letter, 73

Leaders, definition of, 73
    (points), 146
Leading, 34, 40
Leads, definition of, 73
Let-in note, 73
Letter, address and conclusion of, 112
Letterpress, 73
Lettre de forme, 71
Lettre de somme, 71
Ligature, 73
Light-face type, definition of, 73
Line-plates:
    films, 89
    for colored pictures, 90
    for newspapers, 90
    how prepared, 86, 88
    making ready, 91
    printing on the press, 91
    routing, 89
Lists, how punctuated, 95
Locking up, 73
Logotype, definition of, 73

London Journal, 83

MacKellar, Smiths, and Jordan, 21, 27
Macron, the, 146
Make-up of a book, 65
Making ready, 74
Making up, 74
Mapes's Magazine, 83
Marder, Luse, and Company, 27
Master-type, 21
Matrices made by the electrotype process, 23
Matrix, 21, 22
Measurement of type matter, 39
Microscopique type, 33
Missal type, specimen of, 33
Mitchel, William H., 35
Mittel type, 30
Modern-face type, 74
Mould, 22, 23
Moxon, Joseph, 20

Nick, definition of, 74
Nine-point (bourgeois) type, 31
Numbers, how expressed, 95
    how pointed, 112
Numerals, roman and arabic, 95

O and Oh, 117
Octavo, definition of, 60, 74
Odd pages, 74
Old English type, definition of, 66, 74
    specimen of, 33
Old-style type, 75
    modernized, 75

Omission of letters and figures, 123, 134
    of a noun, a verb, or a phrase, 111
Overlay, definition of, 75
Overlays, how prepared, 91
Overrun, definition of, 75
Overrunning, 18, 75

Pagination, 75
Paper:
    bleaching, 49
    book, 56, 59
    calenders, 52
    classes of, 56
    dandy-roll, 50
    deckle-edged, 56, 57
    deckles, 50
    driers, 51
    first machines for manufacture of, 46
    half-stuff, 49
    laid, 54, 56
    loading, 52
    loft-dried, 51
    machine-dried, 51
    preparation of stock, 47
    printing, 56
    shading, 53
    sizes of, 59
    sizing, 52
    staples, 46
    supercalenders, 52
    surface-coating, 53
    water-marks, 50, 64
    wire-cloth, 50
    wove, 54, 56

Paper-writing, 56, 58, 59
Paper-making:
    by hand, 53
    by machinery, 48
Parenthesis, marks of, 124
Parenthetical expressions, 119
    words, phrases, and clauses, 108
Participial and adjective phrases, 109
Penny Magazine, 86 *note*
Period, the uses of the, 94
Petit type, 32
Petrarch, 156
Pi, definition of, 75
Pica type, specimen of, 31
    as unit of measurement of point system, 26, 28
Platen, 75
Points, definition of, 75
Point system, 26
Proof:
    author's, 13, 76
    definition of, 75
    foul, 76
    foundry, 13, 76
    galley, 14, 76
    office, 13, 75
    paged, 13, 17, 76
    plate, 13, 76
    reading, 13
    revised, 17, 76
    second revise, 17
Proof-marks, List of, 1
Proof paper, definition of, 76
Punch, 21, 22
Punctuation marks, 93

Quadrat or quad, 77
Quarto, 60, 77
Quotation marks, the uses of:
    in English, 129
    in French, 163
    in German, 167
    in Latin languages, 131
    in Spanish, 172
        position of points employed with closing, 133
Quotations or extracts, 95, 97, 122, 129, 148

Recto, definition of, 77
Reference marks, 144
Register, definition of, 77
Robert, Louis, 46
Roman type, definition of, 77
    specimens of, 33, 77
Rosenberg, Frederick, 35
Ruby type, 32
Runic type, specimen of, 33

Saint Augustine type, 30
Sauer, Christopher, 20
Script, definition of, 78
    specimen of, 33
Sections, 64
Semicolon, the uses of the, 100
Separatrix, 78
Separatum, 78
Series, words in a, 103
Serifs, definition of, 78
Seven-point (minion) type, 32
Shank, definition of, 78
Sideheads, 95, 122
Signatures, 64, 78

Six-point (nonpareil) type, 32
Sixteen-point (Columbian), 30 *note*
Size notation of American Library Association, 63
Skeleton type, definition of, 79
Slug, definition of, 79
Small capitals, definition of, 79
Solid, 79
Sorts, definition of, 79
Spaces, definition of, 79
Spanish alphabet, 169
Stanhope, Lord, 82
Stars, Three, 146
Stereotyping, methods of, 81, 82
Stock, definition of, 79
Subject and predicate, 110
Superior characters, 79
Sweinheym and Pannartz, 77
Syllabication:
    in English, 140
    in French, 164
    in German, 167
    in Italian, 175
    in Spanish, 172

Take, definition of, 79
Ten-point (long primer) type, 28, 31
Thin-face type, specimen of, 33
Three-point (excelsior) type, 32
Tilde, the, 146, 171
Title-pages, how punctuated, 96
Titles of books and periodicals, 133, 154
    of books, pictures, etc., 132, 154
    of characters, 133
    of respect, affection, dignity, or office, 151

CPSIA information can be obtained
at www.ICGtesting.com
Printed in the USA
LVHW061202201222
735616LV00005B/7